DESERT STORM *Diary*

An American soldier's personal record of the Gulf War in words and pictures

GEOFFREY FRANKEL

with John H. Nielsen

International Standard Book Number (ISBN): 0-9645356-4-5
Library of Congress Catalog Card Number: 97-071519

M-L

**The Morris-Lee
Publishing Group**

**P.O. Box 218, Rosemont, New Jersey 08556
Tel. 609-397-8538 • Fax 609-397-9275**

DEDICATION

To my brothers in arms, I wish you peace.

ACKNOWLEDGEMENTS

First of all, I would like to thank John Nielsen, who took a mountain of handwritten notes and letters to myself—my diaries—and turned them into a story about coming of age; Steve Smith, art director, The Morris-Lee Publishing Group, for his care and attention in the design of this book; Robert Asman, for his many hours in the darkroom producing the photographic prints; and, last but not least, my wife Jennifer, whose love and support has allowed me to recall and heal my memories of war.

CONTENTS

Foreword

It's been nearly seven years since I picked up two sturdy, beautifully made books with inviting blank pages at a department store in Nuremberg, Germany. I had just been ordered to the Middle East. The books were heavy—with a combined weight of more than twenty pounds—but their wooden covers and wrought-iron latches made them wonderful to look at and hold. They reminded me of the daybooks artists might have carried through Europe in the last century—or, even earlier, of captains' logs; or the dusty volumes one might find in an old monastery.

In a way, my diaries became all of these to me. They were also a form of therapy, a way of coming to grips with my life and the very strong possibility that it might soon end. Even before I shipped out to the Gulf War, my journals and I became inseparable. I lugged them everywhere, initially to small cafes, later through numerous desert encampments. I wrote constantly. And when I was tired of writing, I took photographs or drew pictures of what I saw in front of me and in my mind's eye.

Some may find this kind of obsessive journal-keeping self-absorbed and pretentious, even eccentric. But in my unit, everyone had their eccentricities; ways of expressing themselves, of saying, "I'm me, damn it!" For some, it was wearing underwear printed with Valentine's-day hearts; for others it was refusing to don Army socks; still others kept exotic spices to add to their Army rations, if only to make their food—if not their existence—more palatable.

My own method for sustaining my non-military self was my diaries. They kept me sane and taught me a lot about myself. If nothing else, I learned that sometimes, when you feel like nobody, life is as meaningful as you alone make it.

—Geoffrey Frankel
August, 1997

Day for night—Shrouded by hundreds of oil fires, U.S. troops move into Kuwait on a sunny April afternoon

A Remembrance, Not Just of War, but of Growing Up

Essential baggage—Frankel's journals made the entire trip with him, even though they weighed about 20 lbs

For most of us, war in the Persian Gulf was a television event. We watched, riveted, as tracers lit the night skies over Baghdad and American "smart" bombs destroyed target after target with pinpoint accuracy. This was something new in warfare, a kind of morality play for the electronic age—the prime-time triumph of technology over evil. Central Casting even gave us Saddam Hussein to play the bad guy. It was all too tidy and antiseptic, of course. In the years since, we have learned that the Gulf War had its share of blunders and tragedy. But at the time, it was hard not to accept the obscene analogies to video games we heard on nightly newscasts.

Geoffrey Frankel had a different perspective. He was a 23-year-old medic with the Headquarters Battalion, Division Artillery, of the U.S. Army's First Armored Division during the war. He spent the winter of 1990-1991 living in the Saudi Arabian desert, coping with squalor and facing the possibility of death once the shooting started. Fortunately for the rest of us, he kept a diary in which he recorded the fear, boredom, frustration, anxiety, grief, occasional joy and constant self-searching he experienced during those months.

Frankel's journals are both unique and universal. He was lucky. He lived. As a medic with an artillery unit, he didn't even experience combat first-hand. But the very private emotions expressed in that diary have surely been felt by every young man who ever went to war, from Thermopylae to D-Day to Desert Storm. In these pages we meet an intelligent youth—an artist—on the verge of adulthood. Like so many of us at that age, he cares passionately about the great issues of life. He muses about Love, Beauty, Honor, Existence. But most of us at that age are still immortal. Our futures are boundless, because maturity has yet to teach us otherwise. Frankel's musings are poignant—not just because they are youthful, but because he is confronting himself and his own mortality.

Ex-soldiers will feel at home in these pages. They'll learn, for example, that KP still stinks, that latrine duty in the desert means burning shit, and that modern field rations are every bit as disgusting as the chow in other wars. The language and preoccupations of Frankel and his comrades-in-arms are as fresh as today and as old as warfare. Indeed, their experiences demonstrate beyond doubt that the old saws of military life— "Hurry Up and Wait" and SNAFU ("Situation Normal, All F***** Up"), to cite just two— are eternal truths. Why else would the First Armored Division receive its desert camouflage uniforms *after* the fighting was over?

Desert Storm Diary is not a conventional memoir of war. It is a personal document, fundamentally anti-war, the private odyssey of a reluctant soldier who served his country with honor. Geopolitics and military strategy are barely mentioned—not that the GIs weren't passionately interested in both. But they were isolated in the wilderness for months, and very little information filtered down through the chain of command. Their main sources of news were hungrily devoured radio broadcasts from CNN and the BBC.

Much more to the point, the intimate glimpses of daily life in *Desert Storm Diary* underscore the gulf between reality on the ground and the carefully orchestrated perceptions back home. Consider this confrontation with a public-affairs officer who was looking for troops who wanted to talk to their families—but who informed Frankel that "if I couldn't come up with anything happy to say ... I wouldn't be permitted to say anything at all." His reaction ("That's just great. We wouldn't want anyone to think we're not enjoying this.") skewers much of the "information" that was fed to the American public during the war.

To understand the isolation Frankel and his comrades experienced, one need only cite a few landmark events and compare his journal entries for those days:

• On January 29, 1991, the Iraqi army overran the undefended Saudi coastal town of Khafji. The town was quickly retaken in a counterattack that demonstrated a crucial military fact few strategists recognized at the time: the Iraqi army would dissolve before the U.S. and its allies. Frankel's journal notes only that the long wait for the shooting to start had frayed tempers to the breaking point. And that he got two mail deliveries that day—thanks, no doubt, to divine intervention:

> One of the sergeants ... and I have adopted a ritual for mail that seems to work. We press three fingers together, close our eyes, and recite a silent prayer to the evil god of the postal service. So far so good.

• On February 13, F-117 fighter-bombers hit the Al Firdos bunker in Baghdad, inadvertently killing hundreds of civilians, thanks to a failure of military intelligence. Unaware of the disaster, Frankel's unit was preparing to move to its jumping-off point for the invasion of Iraq. His diary contains a typically thoughtful entry:

> I came here a grown man, but I leave a bigger one. And I'm going to a place where I can expect to grow even more. I have learned things about myself and others that no other place could have taught me. For this reason I shall forever despise and love this place.

• The ground war started on February 24. Military history notes that the First Armored Division was part of the VII Corps, the middle force in the three-pronged allied assault on the hapless Iraqi army. Frankel's personal history notes that he and his comrades were spectators, for the most part, fascinated witnesses to the deadly light shows their unit unleashed at night.

Then they saw the results of those barrages. At a time when people at home were rejoicing in the lightning victory, Frankel and a few friends visited a battlefield. "I wish we hadn't," he writes:

> Driving over a hill we came upon a scene that no one should ever witness. But we deserved to see it. We were the curious ones, we wanted proof. We saw tanks that had been opened like tin cans; trucks still running, as if their drivers were coming back any minute; thousands of dead bodies littering the sand. ...As I looked at the torn and mutilated faces, I could hear the screams, see the pain.

Frankel stayed in the desert another six weeks and saw many such vistas. But he also experienced moments of genuine pathos—the little refugee girl, for example, who asked him to take her picture, or the moving scene when he hands his lunch to a hungry Iraqi woman and her child. Either incident could stand as the book's defining moment.

War may not be a good place to grow up, but Frankel did it well.

—John H. Nielsen

Route of the First Armored Division—Frankel's unit was part of VII Corps, the army's main attacking force in the allied sweep through Iraq

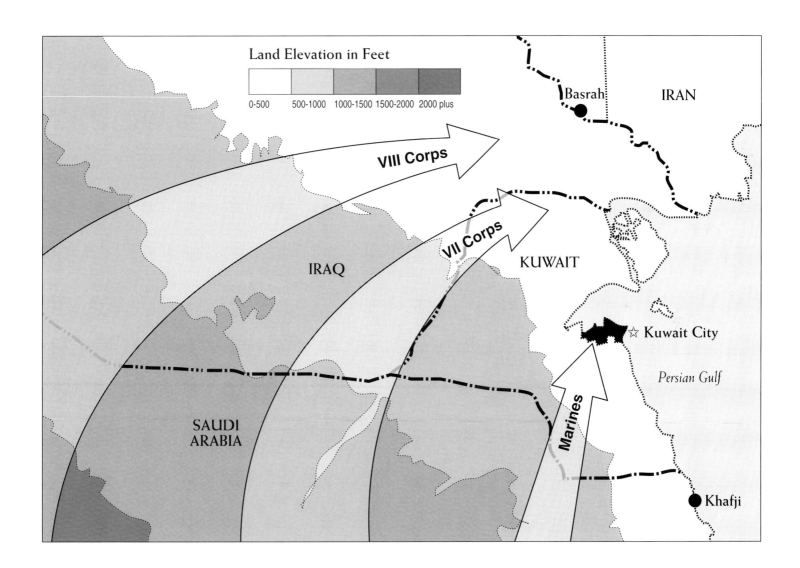

Land Elevation in Feet

0-500　500-1000　1000-1500　1500-2000　2000 plus

Basrah

IRAN

VIII Corps

VII Corps

IRAQ

KUWAIT

Kuwait City

☆ Kuwait City

Persian Gulf

SAUDI
ARABIA

Marines

Khafji

PART ONE

Watch That First Step. It's a...

November 27, 1990. It's 0715 Tuesday morning, no doubt the first of many days to come filled with confusion, vagueness and thwarted ambitions—all because of an approaching misfortune—my involvement in a thing called Desert Shield.

A few hours ago, I was informed that I will deploy to the Middle East. I'm not really sure why I am going or what will be expected of me. I've been paying close attention to what is happening in Iraq. I know that Saddam Hussein has a history of doing inhuman things. I also know that what he has done and is doing to the people of Kuwait—and even to his own people—is wrong. Still, I can't say that I believe in our country's participation. Other foreign governments have inflicted worse misfortunes on their people. Why now? Why there? Why me? I am confused and scared. I am not the gung-ho type. When I enlisted I thought that if there ever was a good reason for me to defend my country, I would. Now my entire future has been put on hold, and I have yet to hear a reason that would make me feel any better.

My mind is spinning. I want to fall asleep and wake up in a different reality. This is uncharted emotional territory. I find it hard to put my thoughts into words.

I am 23. Through a combination of lies, drugs, burned bridges and various misdemeanors, I have wound up in the U.S. Army. Now I'm facing the blunt reality that I may die. It's one thing to risk one's life indirectly by crossing the street or boarding an airplane. It's another to throw the dice in a game with no winners. Politicians are the only

Which way to the mall?—A staging area in Saudi Arabia two shopping days before Christmas

1

players in this game, and they're playing with other people's lives. I wonder if they realize the magnitude of what they're doing.

I'm sitting in a cafe and have just said, "I'll have a coffee please." Those simple words will scream in my memory when I'm thousands of miles from here.

May my inner resources—and whatever gods actually exist—see me through this thing. May I emerge from this ordeal as a whole, free-thinking individual, with my mind and body intact.

I view myself as existing for myself, with myself, to pay for or profit from my own actions. I will soon be entering circumstances in which I will have to rely on those around me for survival—and I wouldn't trust many of the people around me with an empty paper bag.

I recently read the notebooks of Leonardo da Vinci, an artist who produced few visual works, but who retains my deep respect. He lived solely for the love of seeing, documenting, expressing and experimenting with everything around him. I would like to do the same.

I wrote this following segment after spending ten hours in an art museum:

An image to most, is simply a picture.
To me it is a world in which I live,
Until I look away.

It looks as if we are to ship out around Christmas. I hope that we leave after the holidays—not just for my peace of mind, but for the sake of those with families.

I'm floundering in an overwhelming wave of reality. I am going to the Middle East, a place where I will have to shoot at others, and they will be shooting at me!

November 28, 1990. With my luck we will leave on Christmas day.

I read the following quote today. It rings a chime with me. "If the human brain were to be so simple that we could understand it, we would be so simple that we would not."[1]

I have two or three remaining weekends before I depart. Maybe I will be a part of Saddam Hussein's Desert Christmas.

Fatal scrawl—Graffiti left behind by the enemy shows the Iraqi flag and an AK-47 rifle. The painted message reads "Martyrs... are more generous than us all"

2

Every soldier in this unit seems to have an opinion about what will and will not "go down" in Iraq.

Deeply attached to their assumptions, they plan, pack, secure, adjust and readjust their belongings, themselves, their lives, families and futures. They're all convinced that when they've completed these chores, they'll be prepared. Is it possible for a human being to be "ready" to kill and be killed? Those who say they are must be lying to themselves and the rest of us. Their minds must be preparing for what their bodies will be forced to do. They're blocking out their true feelings.

All through basic training I kept a journal of the emotions, thoughts and major events that shaped my days. It should prove interesting later on to compare basic training with Desert Shield—both new experiences capable of altering, even damaging, the one thing that I truly value: my mind! I'm only truly happy when I'm using my talents to express myself. All that I ever desired to learn was the arts. I'm pleased with who I am and with my life—though not necessarily what I've done with my life.

This morning was one of confusion and military-sponsored mayhem. We rushed, ran, strained and confused ourselves as we loaded our military vehicles onto a train for transport to Saudi Arabia. They'll wait there for us.

My fellow soldiers crammed everything but the kitchen sink onto the trucks. People were bringing gallons of tanning oils and cases of Chapstick. It was impossible to find Chapstick in the PX. Footlockers full of the stuff are headed for Saudi Arabia! People forget it's cold in winter, even in the desert.

Others opted for more creative packing—lounge chairs, umbrellas with beer advertisements printed on them, stereo systems, TVs, VCRs, golf clubs, even a motorcycle were among the unauthorized cargo. I guess everyone thought that if they were going to a place where these things don't exist, they should bring them. It certainly makes sense to me. I packed enough books to open a library.

I'm surprised by how well people in the unit are getting along. Before this event, it was hard to find—let alone converse with—my fellow soldiers. Anything more than a hello was seen as a commitment. The prospect of going to war has awakened a sensitivity. We're beginning to realize that the best way to return together is to enter this together.

I just got a letter from my girlfriend here in Germany. The news of my going to war is affecting her more than it has affected me. So far. It's hard for me to express to her what I am going through.

Since I found out that I am going to the desert, my artistic outlets have been cut off. My ideas and creative impulses are trapped in the womb.

I began writing about five years ago. I've long since lost my first journal. Too bad. I had been exploring my mental makeup in it; now it's a missing part of my life. Confiding your thoughts, emotions, ideas—your total self—to a journal is much like having an imaginary childhood friend. But it's more rewarding, because people don't stare. And there's something extraordinary about time spent with yourself—time purposely set aside to explore areas that are normally dormant. When these thoughts are ignored, they atrophy, and die.

I usually don't enjoy waiting, but in this circumstance, I'd be willing to wait a long time. Maybe we'll be stood up. Who's in a hurry to die?

It's strange how I'm living a charade of my normal life, while I wait for something that makes all men cringe—WAR, the ultimate conflict in which men prove their manhood by defending their country. What a crock! All we're really doing is defending our fellow man from other men who are attempting to prove their manhood by challenging us to stop them—all of it initiated by two men who couldn't be farther from the battle.

"If war is horrible, isn't patriotism the dominant idea that supports it?" [2]

I am waiting out this moment at a quaint little cafe in a village down the road from our barracks. The lighting in this place reminds me of those blur filters they put on video cameras. You know, the type used for filming weddings and ice shows. This place serves the best coffee I've ever tasted. It is served with a small butter cookie and a chocolate mint. All placed on a decorative doily. Try to top that at your local diner.

I get a special joy from watching people in the cafe. Each individual approaches his daily rituals differently. People seem to pay little attention to the way they drink a cup of coffee, talk with their hands, play with items on the table or toss about as they laugh in response to something funny. I don't know these people, but I sense that I'll miss them.

I was born in the wrong era. I could really have thrived in the fourteenth to sixteenth centuries. I would have loved to spend sleepless nights pondering the founding principles of art as we now know them. Enunciating the theories that would change the way all future artists express themselves—that would have been an honor.

I don't want to leave this cafe at closing time. I'll miss having whole days to myself. I'll miss long walks with no destinations. The only thing the Army can't deprive me of is my imagination. I need to spend as much time by myself as possible before I go to Saudi Arabia. It will prepare me for the time when all I will have to be entertained with is myself.

We have spent more time packing and unpacking in accordance with constantly changing packing lists than any other preparations so far. It seems to me that the importance of whether four socks go into bag number one and the remaining three pairs go into the second bag or vice versa, is not worth the attention these people are giving it.

I think I'll boycott my girlfriend this weekend. I can't handle the bad attitude she has about my leaving. I think she actually feels worse about it than I do—at least at this stage. She can see the big picture—what will happen if I die, or get injured, or simply return with a large mental scar. I try not to think about those things. If I did, I wouldn't be able to function. The few remaining weeks I have to get a grasp on my situation would become a Hell. I have strong emotions for this woman, but the circumstances make her a threat to me. I only hope that before I leave I'll find the words—and the courage—to tell her why I behaved this way.

It's best that I'm far from my family. The distance acts as an anesthetic. If I were home, the scene would be ugly. I've tried to talk to others in order to gain insights into how they are handling their separations. All I have received are short, superficial responses that tell me nothing. I guess some things are too painful to talk about.

I witnessed the following event on a subway in town: The passengers were bored, reduced to examining other people on the train. Then a little girl riveted the attention of every soul on that car as she twisted and twirled around the center pole. She laughed and screamed herself dizzy—celebrating life, exploring the unknown and expressing herself with utter abandon. Contemplating her innocently beautiful actions, I lifted my smiling face and saw that every other passenger was also grinning. As we shared that momentary smile, it was clear to me that all of us wanted to relive at least one moment when our lives were that important.

"You are worried about seeing him spend his early years in doing nothing. What! Is it nothing to be happy? Nothing to skip, play, and run about all day long? Never in his life will he be so busy again." [3]

November 29, 1990. I'm seated in yet another cafe in yet another German town. Where I am isn't important. What is important is why. I come to these cafes to remind myself that I still can. I want to stamp the special joy I receive from these places upon the walls of my memory. Soon I'll give anything to be here. And memories are our most precious possessions. I am sure I'll find myself reliving these moments when reality becomes too harsh.

I'm not exactly sure who, what or why I am—but I'd like to believe that I'm too important to end up as a statistic in war. I admire those who have died for our country, but I feel uncomfortable about joining them.

The following is a statement that Vasari wrote in his *Lives of the Artists*:

Occasionally, heaven sends us someone who is not only human but divine, so that through his mind and the excellence of his intellect we may reach out to the heavens.

May my writings avoid imitating others! If any of what I have written resembles another's, it was not the work that was shared. We simply traveled the same road. When two or more people travel the same path to knowledge and experience, unless they are traveling parallel, they are sure to cross. When I travel a creative path, I tend to be oblivious to traffic. I am an accident waiting to happen.

One quality that I feel lends beauty to a person is the length they will go to support what they feel strongly about. I am not sure of my feelings about this conflict. I know some who feel quite strongly about giving up their lives for this cause. I have talked to soldiers who are aware of the Why and How of it. They know the odds and are willing to die, if necessary. In my eyes they are beautiful people. They believe that their country is worth the ultimate price. When I think about it, so do those we call our enemies! Someone will be paying too much. Who's right? Who's wrong? Is the winning side automatically on the side of truth? I am frightened! I want to save my life for something I believe is worthy of it. I am a human first, and an American—a very frightened American—second!

November 30, 1990. Another cafe, another town. This place is quite small. It has just four tables with matching chairs, a bar and a door, awkwardly placed at the top of a stairwell. I feel very comfortable here. I was meant to find this place. The evening is young, most people are still bustling about the narrow streets, searching for stuff to enrich their lives. (Can anything really do that?) I'm on another kind of quest—through myself, my mind, my emotions. I'm looking for any hint that I'll be able to cope with war. I once thought that a war was the last thing I would ever have to face. Wrong! And I have no idea how I'll react, endure, even survive. There are countless books that tell you how to prepare physically. I've yet to find one that helps mentally.

The waiter told me that the cafe just opened five minutes ago. He went on to ask where I was from, where I have been, where I was going, and if I was lost. I looked at him and said "I know where I am, you do not want to know where I am going, and you have no idea how lost I really am."

If—or rather when—I survive this experience, I should be stronger for the experience, much more able to control my own destiny. Of course, the first thing to do is survive.

"O' human stupidity! Do you not perceive that you have spent your whole life with yourself, and yet are unaware of the thing you chiefly possess, that is your folly.

"And you fancy that you have wrought miracles when you have spoiled the work of some ingenious mind and do not perceive that you are falling into the same error as he who strips a tree of its adornment of branches laden with leaves intermingled with fragrant flowers or fruit in order to demonstrate the suitability of the tree for making planks."[4]

Soon we'll destroy all of our surroundings—and, in turn, ourselves.

Being sent to Saudi Arabia to fight a war, is an act of rape. I'm surely more than cannon fodder. But when I think about it, I condoned the act when I enlisted.

I feel it is important for me to keep a record of all I see, feel and think—even of little things that might seem irrelevant. To explore what I will become, I must make a picture of who I am now.

An artist is a creature motivated to do what he does by an internal overdrive—an obsession. Most respond to the shifting desires of the moment; artists are chained by necessity.

It's evening. I'm at a pizza place across the street from my studio. It's my home away from home. I come here to act, say and be who I am. I adore this temporary feeling of

Greetings from Saddam—As it turned out, the Kuwaiti oil fires posed the greatest military threat of the war, if only to Allied lungs

8

comfort and sense of belonging. The owner treats me like a son. I'll finish my tomato soup and grappa, then walk. I want to get lost, find a cafe where I can sit and write about my losses and discoveries.

I walked for two hours, till I wasn't sure I had feet. I escaped the cold by slipping into a strange but warm cafe. My fingers are numb and stiff as I write. The place is full of kids who are still young enough to thrive on being alive. They have choices—they can do or be whatever they desire. This group has chosen to save the world from violence. They discuss, plan and project—though neither their bodies nor their ideals ever leave the table.

I have returned to the barracks. It's time to sleep. Every day I have to ask myself what may happen to me, and I've grown to fear the answers. Even if I escape physical damage, I could end up with mental scars.

December 1, 1990. This is a confession to myself. I honestly don't know how I'll react to being shot at. It would be a lie to say that I could automatically respond in a correct military manner. I'm no Rambo. I'd like to believe that I'd be coherent enough to seek protection or defend myself. I may overload my brain and freeze my body, surrendering to the source and ending the pain. I might freak out. I don't know how I will deal with that kind of situation. I hope I never learn.

December 2, 1990 I am at my favorite cafe. I feel pretty good today. How can I feel content and calm so close to the most dangerous crisis of my life? For some reason, I'm experiencing a sort of oneness with myself. I attribute it to the self-exploration in my journals. Writing seems to take away the pain, leaving a sense of accomplishment in its place. I prefer to think about survival, not death.

December 4, 1990. It's only been a week since I began writing in this journal. It seems I've been doing it all my life.

It appears we will not depart until January 1, 1991. What a way to begin a new year. I wonder what the new year has in store for me. My New Year's resolution: Not to Die!

The Chaplain's quote for the day is, "Where there is room for improvement it will always be the largest room."

Here is an area in which I need improvement: Love! Is it really attainable? Or is it like heaven? Everyone talks about it and how they envision it to be. They live on the idea that it exists. But does anyone really know? We die with the same ambition that kept us alive—Hope.

Being "all you can be" is fine if all you can be is the Army. I can be a lot more!

I often wonder how other people see the world around them. I feel everything I see as if it were a painting or a motion picture. Each moment—each frame—enhances the meaning for those that follow, as if life were a story. I just hope I don't miss anything by falling asleep or getting popcorn.

Earth would be a divine place if we could live somewhere else.

The following poem was written by Flan, a close friend:

> For years we have trained for the event of war.
> Now it looms over us like a smoking volcano.
> For the most part we are all children.
> Some are parents who may never again see their children.
> All of us go forward with the fear that we may never return to our loved ones.
> We may never hold our parents or children again, yet we do what we must.
> Those of us who have chosen to be soldiers cannot walk away from our duty.
> We all have different reasons involved in the choice we made.
> The same fears that cause us to wish we could hide, are the same that propel us forward.
> The love for our families and the hope of a safe return is all we have.
> We are willing to sacrifice our own safety for those we love. Yet deep inside we wish we could remain behind in that safety.
> Someone must go, we have stepped forward with hesitant determination to see this through.
> You may ask us why. You may even expect it of us.
> We ask only that you understand we do it for you as well as for ourselves.
> Yet deep inside we wish we could remain behind in unworthy for we tried.
> If we come home to you as someone else, try to understand.
> Do not shun us.
> Try to make us feel we can be proud of what we do.

In the end we did it out of love.
Love for our families, for our country, and for humanity.

I just competed a painful task. Call it the Separation Stage. With the last written line, the last addressed envelope, I put the final check on my list of goodbyes before departure. Is there a proper way to say farewell to your life and those in it? I wonder how I'd respond to receiving such a letter. I stare at the little pile of unhappiness I've constructed, trying to decide if I should cast this pall on my friends and loved ones. Do I have the right? Would it be worse if I didn't? How can my words begin to capture my motives, the depth of my feelings?

These people made me who I am. My letters tell them that their project—me—is no longer available to them. Thanks anyway. Please keep in touch. I'm about to leave, to cast off the lines that hold me to the shore—to the edge, that is, of my known world.

I am who I am with no choice. I am only able to make myself the best me I am capable of becoming. Can one ask for a more divine inner peace than to enjoy being oneself?

"Oh, excellent thing, superior to all others created by God! What praises can do justice to your nobility? What peoples, what tongues will fully describe your function? The eye is the window of the human body through which it feels its way and enjoys the beauty of the world. Owning to the eye and soul it is content to stay in its bodily prison, for without it, such a bodily prison is a torture." [5]

I just returned from the telephone. I stood in a little yellow box and talked to the two people who brought me into the world. As we talked, we knew that we may never speak again. I felt as though our words built a fence around my emotions. I found myself saying things that fell short of expressing what I felt. The English language—or any other—doesn't hold words powerful enough, adjectives expressive enough, to convey my message. I love them that much!

I have had many thoughts lying dormant, hibernating for a long time. There was no reason for them to be called forth. Until now. The possibility of being lost forever has awakened them. Like general-admission seating at a concert, they fight for their place, a permanent position on paper.

This weekend was full of sentimental goodbyes. We have yet to receive a definite date for departure, but everyone senses that it's close. As the weekend slides to an end, the thought that this could be my last time with friends hangs over me like a great weight. Arms embrace, tears fall, promises take flight, knowing they will never be kept.

Receiving such heartfelt farewells was touching and memorable, even though I believe we'll meet again. Our date of departure has made more moves than I can count. Every time I must put my friends through this farewell routine I feel like the boy who cried Wolf.

PART TWO

Crying Wolf—Endlessly

December 9, 1990. Monday morning, and it's time to venture out into 12-degree weather.

It's obvious to all of us that we've crossed the line. We can neither turn back nor cancel this conflict. In the beginning, I thought it would resolve itself or be over before I joined it. Now we're in the grip of a kind of predatory inertia. People have been letting off steam any way they can. Some get drunk in town. Others have turned to each other. Friendships have sprouted everywhere. People who never talked to each other seek shelter in a stranger's heart. We all possess common fears. In boundless conversations, soldiers spill the contents of their emotions onto the floor and find some solace.

"Let the festivities begin!" That's how we felt after a warning briefing tonight from our Command Sergeant Major (CSM). He didn't use a conference room or a large formal assembly. He had the sensitivity the moment demanded. At night he came into our barracks, a place which is normally a circus after five o'clock. There was no shouting out of orders or knocking on doors. Even in our rooms we felt his presence. We gathered in our socks and underwear, toting ashtrays and cigarettes. We opened our ears, but he already had our hearts. His face told us what he had difficulty saying: that we'd be leaving very soon. He apologized on behalf of the Army for denying us what could possibly be our last Christmas. He told us that he wanted us to make sure we were ready. When finished, he lowered his head, patted a few of us on the back and made his way through the

An army travels—The First Division moved tons of vital war materiel during Desert Shield, including these lawn chairs

15

touched crowd of soldiers. Then, as if possessed, we all began partying—drinking beer and acting silly. I am conscious of my actions, but my subconscious mind is already in the sand.

Now I'm sitting, tense and alone. Fear and anger have caught up to me. I honestly can't predict what I'll do when "the shit hits the fan." I look at myself and wonder how my mind will steer my body through the traffic ahead. I scan my soul seeking answers. How can I kill another? As humans, we are all brothers. My involvement may force me to murder or mutilate. I'll be destroying lives—not just those of my victims, but of all who are affected by my actions.

We're not the judges or the jury. How can we be the executioners? Is it right just because one man says so, because we happen to be wearing the colors of the week? It should not and must not be that simple! Deep down, we're aware of the various reasons that make each of our enlistments unique. Still, it was written on the paper we signed. Were we really made aware of the possible reality? Now I am able to see that reality clear as day. To kill countless innocent people—or be killed by them. Have we all forgotten that we are human beings? We've been given the gift of life! It was given so we may learn, grow and enjoy living. None of us came into the world with instructions, but we should have. The instruction should read, "Do not enrage. Product may cause harm to itself and others. Some assembly required—and a lot of parental guidance!"

December 11, 1990. The briefing by the CSM and the celebration that followed were premature. We have about a week left until we fly.

It's one thing to write about fears you once had or may encounter. It's different when you're actually writing scared.

With each passing day I find myself having difficulty staying afloat. The rippling waves of the military are tossing me blindly back and forth. I only hope the ripples aren't whipped up into a storm.

I'm now seated at what is known to "barracks rats" as the Base Club. Its main sources of entertainment are cheap beer and whiskey. Lack of cash, desire, companionship and

Flan—Poet, backwoods philosopher, friend

16

vision enslave the inhabitants of this wasteland. My own self-worth wasn't enough to carry me past its doors. Tonight is like any other here—though at the same time tonight is like no other. Every single person here shares the same fear and the same destiny. We're drinking together in preparation.

If I die and come to rest in Arlington National Cemetery, I don't want an American flag posted on my grave. I ask this not because I am anti-American, but because of this: If I were strolling down the street and suddenly hit by a taxicab, it would make sense not to have a photo of the taxi or its driver on my headstone. Am I right? In this spirit, I make my request.

December 12, 1990. I'm back at my favorite cafe. I've been here for quite a while. I can't bring myself to leave. This place has been an incubator of thoughts. The idea of never returning hurts. I feel mentally empty and emotionally stuffed.

I write as often as I did when I began this journal, but I fill fewer pages. Every morning and evening I sit down with my journal, and together we explore many things. All I had to do to start a lengthy entry was expose a page. Now I have difficulty translating anything into words. As time passes, I'm sure to get lost between the lines.

I feel a bit ill—not physically, emotionally. The invisible weight of this confrontation is affecting me the way the bends affect a deep-sea diver. I'm ready to explode. The torture is too great!

An advance party left for Saudi Arabia last night.

December 14, 1990. Lives are like puzzles. You're born with a complete one, then as you grow it is taken away from you piece by piece. When you reach adulthood, only a fraction of your puzzle remains. You spend your whole life trying to find the missing pieces. Some try to make a life out of the few they still have, but they're never able to construct a recognizable image. If you're motivated to seek out the missing pieces, you stumble across the world picking up bits that don't quite fit. You have grown and changed. So have the spaces that were left unfilled. It will always appear impossible to construct a complete image of who you are. This is what keeps us going. If you have or know someone who has one of my pieces, please tell them to give it back to me.

December 15, 1990. We've been told that we'll depart Monday or Tuesday at the latest. Today is Friday. That gives us one weekend. How can I enjoy it, knowing it's my last? I'll be overcautious with everything I do. I'll try too hard to make every little thing perfect. How can I enjoy myself knowing that the memory of this weekend has to last indefinitely?

This journal, a pack of cigarettes, and a cup of cappucino are all I need. I am in the eye of the storm, about to be hurled into mayhem. My mind is creating thoughts my hand cannot illustrate.

December 16, 1990. Some people have been quite blunt in their sincerity as they say goodbye to me. They must fear that they'll never see me again.

Today I feel crazy, restless. I want to do something wild. But what? There isn't much to do in this town. If this is to be my last weekend of uninhibited release, I'd rather be in a city accustomed to such behavior.

Due to the previous delay of our departure I was able to talk with my parents again. We talked for almost an hour. We chatted about nothing important. The fact that we were talking was very important.

December 17, 1990. I spent most of last night at a ritzy cafe savoring precious moments with friends. A waiter asked me how I felt about going to war. He wanted to know how I was dealing with leaving my friends and family to go far away and into danger. I didn't have time for long explanations, but I kept as close to the truth as I could. I asked him to place his hand on the table and leave it still, no matter what happened. He agreed. I then proceeded to lower my burning cigarette closer and closer to the back of his hand. I had no intention of stopping. It was a good thing he decided I must be crazy. He moved his hand. I don't have to worry about answering any more questions from him.

I've built up an intense anger through all the confusion, uncertainty, and Boy Who Cried Wolf rehearsals. I do not want to go! But if we must go, let's get there already! Anything is better than this purgatory. As a result of yet another delay, I have one more day to spend as I like. I thought last night was my last. I celebrated with friends. We embraced, cried, shared and mourned. We were sure that this was absolutely our last time together. Now I have one more day and no more money. I don't dare call or visit any of my friends. They think I'm gone. Contacting them would be like running into a pallbearer at your funeral. I refuse to call out in fear of that damn wolf again. No one will come. I sit alone—sad, impatient and scared out of my skin.

This extended delay has sucked out all of my drive, not to mention my patience.

December 18, 1990. With less than twenty-four hours before our alleged departure, I'm counting the thin strands of sanity that hold me together. Talk about stage fright! I'm beside myself. Why did I join a company that puts on this type of performance?

Tonight is the last evening we'll have in civilization for a long time—or forever. I keep using the term "forever." I've learned to respect that word. It means more to me now than ever before. Over the past three weeks, I've had to handle totally new emotions. I'm able to look back on how I handled certain stages of my deployment. I've noticed that I and others have tried to appear as if we were doing all the right things to prepare for it. There were many procedures to ensure that our possessions and loved ones would be cared for in case of the worst. Some made car payments, apartment payments. Some even had to teach their wives how to drive or show them where the buses would pick them up. There were many classes for families of departing soldiers—check writing, car care, cooking, even child care. We had to pack our belongings into boxes. We did this so that if we die, the boxes would be sent to our families. No matter how trivial these chores seemed, they had to be addressed. Everyone went through the motions, but no one wanted to recognize what we were doing really meant. We were preparing for death. We have surgically removed ourselves from the planet. This makes sense to me. Murderers shouldn't leave traces behind!

I broke down and called my girlfriend. I feel quite strange about her. Before I was told that I was going to war, we had big problems. Since then, we've put our differences aside. I guess there's no reason to go through all that separation stuff if I'm going to die! We've been together a year, one week from today. She gave me a little present with instructions not to open it until I get to Saudi Arabia. I opened it anyway, in case it was something I'm either not allowed to bring or do not want to be caught bringing. This might sound strange, but in basic training my friends let their sense of humor get away from them. They sent me a battery-operated dildo, knowing very well that whenever a soldier in basic training receives a package, it is opened by the drill sergeants. I had a rough time convincing the sergeants that my friends were joking.

Another statement from my friend Flan: "Sometimes I would be doing something, and I would have to sit and think. My mind would spurt off in many directions. I would think of simple things like my son's first tooth. I was not there for that. How many more precious moments will I have to miss? Will I ever be able to take him to the dentist? If he had no cavities I would say 'That's great, let's go get an ice cream sundae and rot your teeth.' Most of all I am concerned about my mother. If something happens to me, it would surely kill her. My sister died a month before her twenty-fifth birthday. My twenty-fifth birthday is this spring. I must make it to age twenty five. That is the biggest milestone in my life. I have to reach it. Twenty-five or bust!"

Of all the chores that I've completed, none was as important—or as devastating—as filling out my will. It's one thing to make a will as a precaution. That's a gesture of caring and responsibility. It's a totally different story filling one out because you might soon die. Most people can adjust their wills as they grow older, acquire more things or simply change their minds. I have to get it right the first time. Until today, I did every thing to avoid death. Here, on a single piece of paper, I had to plan for it. All other chores seemed to beat around the bush. This will was the bush. It was a step I never saw coming. After tripping over the will, I may continue to stumble until I fall flat on my face in sand.

Tonight, those of us in the barracks have grown close, very close. Being together to enjoy the last evening is the only thing that keeps us from an evil, lonely torture.

Being an artist—and I'm The Artist around these parts—I'm normally seen as one of "them," not one of "us." Tonight the fear of being nobody has made every one "us." I've been adopted by a group of guys as "a cool dude," for two reasons: First, I can draw ("That's cool that you can do that, man"); second, I've done more drugs than all of them put together.

Once again, I'm at my favorite cafe, having scraped up enough cash for a two-way trip and a cup of coffee. If I run out of cigarettes I'm in trouble. The urge to get out of the barracks and run to "home base," was strong, stronger than whatever is gripping those who remain in the barracks.

"Men love war because it allows them to look serious. Because it is the one thing that stops women laughing at them."[6]

December 19, 1990. It's 0945. We're just hours from departure. It will probably be another false alarm. The guys around me seem like people about to visit a haunted house. Some are scared; others are curious. Then there are those who enjoy the thrill it.

Everyone knows exactly where we're headed, but no one acts as if we're going to war. This might be a result of the confusion over our departure date, though I don't think so. The way people are acting is a shock. It feels like we're going on a big field trip with enough picnic lunches to last for months.

As much training as we have received and as much as we think we're physically and mentally prepared, we are still in for a rude awakening.

We leave in an hour. Wives are giving and receiving hugs that must symbolize all that two people feel toward each other. That's impossible, but it will have to suffice. So the last embraces are rendered, the last hands waved, and we cram into the buses. Destination: Hell.

As we climb aboard, the Division's band plays a patriotic song. Yes! A band. You can't go to war without a band! I think I'm going to be sick—on the band.

The bus is far too small for all of us and our gear. Is this symbolic of how we'll spend what might as well be an eternity?

As we inch closer to where I wish not to go, it becomes hard for me to use soft and natural words to describe this journey. There is nothing natural or soft about sending more than half a million children into a war—a war that will no doubt prove that our father has access to the better firecrackers. Yes, children! Most of us have yet to become what we want to be when we grow up.

We're now on the airplane. I was peering around, amazed at what I witnessed (which I'll describe in detail later) when I noticed that the man next to me seemed to be somewhere else emotionally. I asked what was wrong and said, "I know that this is a painful step, but we will make it through." Lifting his head slowly, fighting the pressures against it, he answered, "As I left home this morning I asked my son Andrew to do me a big favor. I asked him to take care of his Mommy and his sister while I was gone. He was disappointed, but agreed. He then added that he will miss me very much and said 'Daddy, I want to come to the desert. I can help you fight the bad men.' I said, 'Andrew the bad men are very mean and they might hurt you.' He answered, 'It's OK daddy, I've got my mean Ghostbuster jammies on.'"

PART THREE

The Spiritual Gypsy Camp and Chutzpa Filling Station

The following is a statement from my friend Flan. He was the last person to leave Germany for Saudi Arabia. Here he describes what it was like being left behind to deal with the emptiness.

"It was so hard being the last person to leave for the desert. There are forty rooms up on our section's floor. After everyone left there was no one. Just me and those long, empty, silent hallways. There were people down on the first floor, but that was a world away. There was only one person in the office to answer phones, but who's going to call? There was nobody to talk to. Walking down the hallway was torture. Before, I'd walk down that hall and hear music coming from someone's room. I'd go in, tell a few jokes, play a little grab-ass and leave. That last night, the only sound in the hallway was my footsteps. They normally wouldn't echo; the acoustics don't allow it. But I swear that I heard them echoing, on and on as if I was in an endless cavern. I was the only one there. The only sounds that I could hear were my heart or my footsteps. Eventually I couldn't leave my room. I needed the security.

"All my friends were gone. People I didn't even like were gone, and it bothered me that they weren't there. Nobody came to bum cigarettes. No one knocked on my door just to call me an asshole. It was a ghostly feeling, eerie. I busied myself with simple things like doling out my belongings, my meager possessions to those on the first floor.

Fill 'er up—Jet fuel began flowing again at Kuwait City's airport after it was recaptured by GIs

'Do you want this table, this chair? Here, take some dishes. Take my trash can, my broom, this mop, some cleanser.' I was giving away my life. If I didn't come back, what good would those things do my mother? I put my life in order to prepare for my death, taken care of all the details. Only two details were left: Where do we bury the son of a bitch, and who gets the cash?"

The atmosphere on the plane is surrealistic. We're not acting like soldiers going to war—at least not the soldiers depicted by Hollywood, which is all most of us have for a reference. I would expect this moment to be much more dramatic or emotionally powerful. The guy next to me is the only one who seems to be acting normally. At least he is crying over his child. I guess I expected everyone to be crying—especially myself.

Maybe it's the flight attendants—yes, flight attendants! Not army women, but beautiful, European Icons. As we pushed by them, one of them said, "As soon as everyone finds a seat, we will begin to serve beverages. Our first film will be *All Dogs Go to Heaven*."

It took a while for everyone to gain a grip on this in-flight circus, but now some have fallen asleep. We've been in the air for about an hour and a half. Some read or listen to music. Others are chain-smoking or walking frantically around the cabin. Some are pestering people. I'm doing a little of each. The only way I could enjoy this flight is if it were going somewhere else.

The pilot just announced that since we took off he has been asked to marry two soldiers to a couple of his flight attendants. He also said that he was asked to perform one divorce.

This is definitely not your normal airline flight, though I guess the scenes in this plane have their own bizarre logic. Near the emergency exit, three gorgeous Icons are examining a M16 rifle. When was the last time I saw flight attendants admiring a passenger's semi-automatic weapon?

Another group of Icons is gathered around an MRE (Meal Ready Eat. I think that most of them were cooked and packaged before I was born.). They're picking at its covering and daring each other to open it. This trip is not unlike taking a limousine full of booze and women to an execution.

The Icons control the atmosphere and tension levels on the plane with ease. To them, this flight goes far beyond just a job. They realize this is the best treatment that any of us will receive for a long time—or forever. But it still feels like a field trip to me. I hope we are going to the zoo. I love the zoo!

Almost everyone is asleep, enjoying themselves in their dreams. The fantasies, even the nightmares they might be experiencing are nothing compared to the nightmare that is awaiting them.

War is not fought by men, it makes them.
Only boys willingly go to war,
Wars that are started by men with boyish behavior.

Our flight, which we wish had lasted even longer than it seemed, has landed on Saudi soil—or, more accurately, Saudi sand. All the prayers that we'd somehow be saved from actually arriving have gone unanswered. Let the nightmare begin.

I am now seated in a Salvador Dali painting. Any minute, I expect to see a giraffe or elephant on fire with a telephone wrapped around its neck.

I am sitting on my duffel bag, searching for something to focus on. There is nothing! I am looking as far as my eyes can see—which is very far—and I see absolutely nothing. This place is going to give me a new definition of that word. Nothing.

I helped—or should I say I was ordered to help—unload the baggage from the belly of the beast that brought us here. I have been in Saudi for about twenty minutes, and I'm ready to leave, if only I could find my return ticket. But while I'm here I might as well try to enjoy this winter vacation.

Compared with the winter weather in Germany, it feels warm here. The air is dry, not to mention tense and filled with fright. Due to the heat, we were told to drink as much water as we can, as often as we can. The dry air and heat drains the fluid out of a person at a pace you're unaware of. We were then directed to the water. Never in my life have I ever seen so many crates of bottled water—or anything else, for that matter. We attacked the mountain like an army of fledgling archaeologists, hauling away far more than we could carry.

The situation is this: After a bumpy, two-hour bus ride, we're in a holding area with

Waving banners—One soldier's answer to Desert Storm's most daunting challenge: keeping clean

full bladders and no bathrooms. This is a state of emergency.

Immediately after our mass consumption of water, we were stampeded onto makeshift tourist buses. We sat for 50 minutes before the drivers even started the engines. I was in the back of my bus, behind a structure of wood and metal meant to separate men and women. With everybody feeling like water balloons, the bus finally lurched away from the airport and toward chaos. About halfway there, everyone—no ranks excluded—began to feel the oncoming terror. Personal modesty vanished. In the great army tradition of leadership by example, one captain grabbed an empty water bottle and relieved himself in it. That started a chain reaction, which went quite smoothly until we passed a car whose occupants could see us through the back door—which, of course, was mostly glass. Suddenly, our gigantic, rolling lavatory was as shocking to us as it was to our Arab spectators. A few laughs were exchanged and a couple of faces turned various shades of red, but our eyes were no longer yellow.

I now write from what I can best describe as a gypsy camp. When we arrived, all I could see was nothing in every direction. Now I'm surrounded by tents, trucks, makeshift bathroom facilities—and people.

This feels more like a Grateful Dead concert than a war. People are walking around as if they're happy to be here. That is either a misconception on my part, or I've finally snapped. I suppose this is a better place to be than out in the middle of Iraq. If I must stay here a while I might as well find a place to fit in this catbox from Hell. This might be an interesting place to visit, but I wouldn't want to defend it.

I'll try to share an experience that sums this place up. On my first trip to the latrine, I followed the directions—past numerous tents, along strange new paths, and around holes in the sand. Suddenly I found myself confronting a wooden box. I had set out to find a bathroom; I ended up realizing that I was in for some major adjustments. I entered to find a toilet seat nailed to a smaller box. On the wall was some reading material: "The flies that frolic on your feces today, may dance on your dinner tomorrow." Not exactly a proverb, and certainly no Zen implications that I could make out. After a moment's contemplation, I concluded that it meant I should close the lid when I finished.

The camp has an odd spiritual feeling that seems to radiate from every tent, every grain of sand. It's as though we're living just outside reality, on a movie set. Someone else is directing all that I see, hear and experience. I'm living a Stephen Spielberg movie I call

The Spiritual Gypsy Camp and Chutzpah Filling Station. There is an emotion in me that I didn't know until I entered this camp. It's hard to write about the sights and sounds and sensations of the place. All I can say is that everything seems fictional. There's a small doubt in my mind that any of this is actually real. In a bizarre way, I feel privileged to be living this experience—though I'll be seriously upset if it ends my life.

I wish I had the energy and ability to describe all that's going on here. It's unreal! This place operates twenty-four hours a day, digesting equipment and soldiers, then spitting them out to fight a war. I'm reminded of the machine in Willy Wonka's laboratories. Looking across the camp at any hour one sees constant movement. The place never sleeps. They say that 20,000 to 40,000 people are here on any given day. I see no reason to doubt it.

It's time to steal some sleep, though that isn't easy, because a sergeant I call Don Quixote keeps mumbling on about his grandchildren and about how stupid his idiot-proof camera is. Don is certainly an interesting person, but right now I don't have the energy to tackle his story. Maybe later.

It's 10:30 P.M. I slept about three hours. I was awakened by all the activity that twenty people in one tent can generate. My mind and spirit seem intact, but my feet are cold.

Isolated in the desert like this, you find yourself asking questions: Why? How? How long? The environment here is so different from anything I've known or read about. We're all here to do something unique in our lives. In a sense—a masochistic sense—we're privileged to be witnessing this. I like to think that if I live through it I will emerge stronger, with a focus in my life that I would never have without the war.

The feeling in the air here is like being on a beach at night. There is a cool breeze from the ocean, sand everywhere, plus that certain isolated stench that is native to such places.

We're scheduled to move to a more permanent camp in a few days. When we do, we'll find out how we'll really live in this country, and we'll begin to search within ourselves for companionship. That should lead us to places in our minds that were previously unknown to us.

All the comforts—Desert Shield meant months of bad meals from mobile kitchens (Page 32) and reluctant visits to semi-public latrines (Page 33). The two hovels on the right were for women

The sounds I hear are of constant preparation with no hint of letting up or slowing down. Every new soldier is fuel for the fire that powers the engine propelling us into war. As I completed that last sentence I realized how quiet it has become in the tent. I'm sitting on my cot with a flashlight and pen tightly grasped in my nervous hands. For a minute I thought everyone had left. Closing my eyes I almost imagined I wasn't here. I should practice that.

December 21, 1990. Today is my second day in Saudi and my first morning. Each soldier is slowly rising with individual style. Some hop straight to their feet; others choose a slower pace. In whatever condition, they drag their water, towels, shaving gear, butts and memories of creature comforts over to the medieval construction entitled the latrine. There they try to restore as much human dignity as conditions permit.

One of the soldiers in our tent was talking in his sleep last night. He was calling out for Sgt. Quixote, who went over to him. "When were we going to stencil our canteens?" the soldier asked. (We don't.) The soldier was quite indignant when Don didn't give him the answer he was looking for. Everybody in the tent woke up this morning with some recollection of the incident. It gave us a healthy laugh.

Today is Friday, though in relation to where we are, and what we're here to do, it's another in an infinite series of Mondays. The days are indistinguishable from each other. There is something unsettling about jumping from being a soldier five days a week, eight hours a day to being a soldier all the time.

We spend our days in this holding area relaxing, preparing and thinking. Right now the guys in my tent are packing and repacking their bags in a valiant effort to cram in more nonessentials. The important thing now is to sneak all that one can into those bags. This will be our last chance to collect and store before we ship out to the next Nowhere.

One unique quality of this place is that there are only nine hours of daylight at this time of year. It makes it hard to achieve all we must in a day. Plus the night fills most of our heads with fear of the future. At least in daylight we're preoccupied by unfamiliar sights.

My new friend Don has a sense of humor and irony that I find compatible and comforting. Don just said "I like conversing with intellectual people, so I talk to myself."

People are spending a lot of their time trying to accumulate friends. A friend you can confide in, trust and discuss your fears with is worth more than a bullet-proof vest around here. Those in pursuit of sexual partners have adopted a signaling method. We all have army flashlights with colored lens filters, each of which has a specific tactical purpose. In this camp, the blue filter has taken on an entirely new meaning.

At dinner Don said, "I wasn't sure that there was a God until I became sure of the fact that there is a devil." Sometimes it surprises me to find so many special people in uniform. I have to remind myself that before they put on Army green, they sported their own colors.

Last night I received a very warm feeling from a conversation with two soldiers. We discussed the earth and skies, war and peace, love and hate. I might have been in a college cafeteria. Then a sandstorm brought me back to reality.

I just returned from guard duty, protecting the camp from enemies in the desert. The irony is that they won't give the guards ammunition. They're afraid that we might hurt someone. Now I have to jump through my ass preparing to leave in the morning, which is only a few hours away. Who needs sleep anyway? I had some last week.

Earlier today I had a chance to wash my hair. I used Prell. The smell reminded me of a girl from my past. Next time that I go to a war I'll remember not to bring things that hold memories of better times.

Don suggested that I keep a daily quote for all who are interested. Good idea. I think I will. Today's quote was "Iron rusts from disuse, stagnant water loses its purity and in cold weather becomes frozen, so does inaction sap the vigor of the mind."[7]

The hours and days have already become an undefined blur. There is no beginning and no end. I can usually see quite far.

PART FOUR

Tent: General Purpose, Medium, One Each

December 22, 1990. After all the confusion of moving out—or of anything else the Army is involved in—we're now in a large convoy. Destination: somewhere in the desert. My rear end is beginning to feel the length of the trip, but I chuckle as I recall some of the unofficial names for our mission: "The Iraqi Horror Picture Show," "Hurry up and Kuwait" and "Saddam's Desert Christmas Show." I just remembered! We have two more shopping days until Christmas.

We've traveled six hours and covered 150 miles. No rest for the impatient. We're scheduled for another 100 miles before we stop.

I see nothing but sand. There isn't a single tree, bush, weed or blade of grass in sight. I could make a drawing of the place by scrawling a single line across the page. Not counting our convoy, the only line out here is the horizon. If we were to "nuke" this place, the world would never run out of glass.

Once again, I am struggling with the thought of how bizarre it is to be plucked out of Western society and landed in this void. I feel uncomfortable in this place, and I feel even stranger being asked to defend it.

Every hour or two the entire convoy stops for a urination break. For males, this entails ducking behind a truck; for females, squatting in the truck with an altered water bottle. At each break soldiers congregate to share thoughts of where we are and where we'll be

A private moment—Mail was a mixed blessing in the desert. It meant a brief, precious glimpse of home, but it also meant exposing emotions best left buried in the daily reality of the desert

living next. I want to know where all the seashells on this beach went. And by the way, where is the damn ocean?

Every mile or two we pass abandoned vehicles on the side of the road. There are oil tankers, buses and wrecked passenger cars. What happened to the people in these wrecks? They'd die before they could reach a gas station—or even a change in contour, for that matter. This whole place looks like a set from Mad Max.

We're no longer passing anything, not even twisted vehicular carnage. To me, this means that no one has ever come out this far, and there must be a reason. When we left the holding area this morning, we left something, a place with people and things. We then headed out across nothing in search of our new home. I suppose that when we reach something, we will have arrived, though I could be wrong. We're turning off from the main road and heading into the void. We're obviously lost. Then again, if we knew where we were going, no one would have enlisted in this damn institution in the first place.

We left the main road in an orderly military manner. Now we look like 200 people in large trucks searching for a lost contact lens.

I know that what I'm here to do has nothing in common with humor, but when you mix people and military regulations, humor is inevitable.

I can't see anyone or anything, but it is evident that there is a large presence out here. I assume this by all the tire tracks in the sand. I also see numerous herds of sheep and goats with no one tending them. What are they eating? I see nothing remotely edible on the sand, not even for those creatures.

We've stopped at what I would like to call just another pit stop. But I'm afraid I'm wrong. I just heard a high-ranking voice say, "This is it." This is it? You must be crazy. We are in the middle of nowhere. This might be something though it can't be "it." There's nothing here!

It's very late. We've thrown ourselves into a few quickly assembled tents and are trying to settle in, as if that were possible. My mind is still showing re-runs of what lies on the other side of this tent. I cannot conceive how vast a nothingness this desert must be. It is difficult to believe that this is real, that we're not being projected into a landscape by Dali.

Back at the Filling Station I began a quote of the day, I'll either post it somewhere or give it to people who ask for it. Tomorrow's quote will be, "An optimist sees only the green light everywhere, while the pessimist sees only the red light, the truly wise person is color blind."[8]

I'm about to turn in. I rest knowing that I'm in possession of all my optimism and self-control. I'm counting on these forces to help me shine a bit brighter and longer than one would expect. With luck, I'll be able to illuminate a few flickering lights along the way.

December 23, 1990. Christmas is only a couple of days away. I believe everyone wishes for the same thing this year.

December 24, 1990. We're spending the day before Christmas observing Yuletide traditions: digging foxholes, filling sand bags and contemplating survival. Isn't that how everyone spends the Holidays?

Today we began the groundwork for the city we'll build in this desert. I don't think we're capable of building anything high enough to escape its origin: Sand!

Four very large bulldozers just arrived. They're supposed to dig a thirty-by seventy-foot hole in our front yard. I was saddened to learn that the hole was for military purposes, not for a swimming pool.

I'm living from day to day. There is nothing to look forward to except leaving. Our real lives are so far in the future that it's hard to keep our heads up.

I should probably get used to going to bed when the sun disappears. It's impossible to continue working. Wakeup time is the moment you don't need a flashlight to tell you it's too early.

This place has already given new meaning to the morning chore of washing up. Washing up once meant running water over my hands so that my mother could hear it. Now it entails a cleansing process that falls just short of involving a blow torch.

I was awakened at 0530 in the blessed A.M., to be informed of my involuntary and mandatory participation in guard duty. We have two, two-hour shifts every twenty-four hours. I'm beginning to dislike the mayor of this city. We have to walk around this infinite nothingness and guard it. Once again to ensure the safety of would-be attackers, we have no ammunition. I guess we're supposed to beat the enemy silly with our rifles, like little old ladies with umbrellas.

December 25, 1990. Christmas. But it feels more like Judgement Day. I feel fragile in this macho-man's land. I have always relied on brains rather than brawn. Out here the reverse is essential.

On the first day of my desert Christmas, Santa gave to me…a lesson in how to dispose of human waste on a vast scale in the desert. The process has acquired the blunt but illustrative nickname of Shit-Burning. The stench of it is not easily forgotten. Neither is the memory of learning how to do it on Christmas day.

Sitting in my new home, a few hours before Christmas dinner, I swallow fear in order to function. We've been split up into four tents: one for officers, another for NCOs, the remaining two for enlisted men. The first of these two tents is occupied by those who consider themselves special. It's good that they're forcing themselves on each other rather than the rest of us. My tent is already called The Ghetto. Its occupants represent a large portion of the world's brands. We sound like a joke. "You have seven colored guys, a Panamanian, three rednecks, and a Jew all living in one tent. One turns to another and…etc., etc."

The instant our tent was up, territorial squabbles began. Everybody grabbed a desirable percentage of the available space. As more and more tenants moved in, our percentages shrank, leaving us barely enough room to stand. The fact that we have little room and a lot of stuff has inspired some creative decorating. Our domicile doesn't remotely resemble anything military. The visual flavor is closer to a Chinese fire drill in mid-transformation. I have already been given the title of landlord. This is due to my space being slightly larger than anyone else's or to my being the only Jew in the "building." We've tossed our possessions onto our cots to mark our territories, like dogs urinating on bushes.

We are scraping the crud off our bodies in preparation for dinner. We'll have plenty of time to decorate later. The soldiers in this tent aren't acquainted yet, but it shouldn't be long before we know each other well. I'm not sure if this will be done smoothly, for a little racial tension is evident. I am sure that over the months we'll grow to respect each other. But there are animosities—and just because of skin tone. We better pull together

Digging in—The troops wanted a swimming pool, but this excavation housed communication trucks

and fast, or we'll all wind up looking the same—dead!

The organizers of this holiday get-together have orchestrated a Christmas dinner for us. It should be interesting to see how people react. It will be our first chance to lighten up since we left Germany. Who knows? The next time might be at Easter—or never! Everybody realizes this. Although we welcome it, we also fear it for the same reasons.

Dinner was pretty good. I actually enjoyed the food, which says a lot considering who manages this restaurant. The highlight was a care package from the "Any Service Member" goodies—cookies, candy, cakes and so on. The gifts were sent by the families of the soldiers in our unit especially for this evening. I'm on Cloud Nine. I was handed a bag of Pepperidge Farm gingerbread men—my favorite. The celebration is still going on as I write from a foxhole on guard duty. I'll be OK, I brought my cookies with me.

After returning to my tent, I began decorating my apartment. I call it that because I have managed to isolate myself from the others as much as possible. I've managed to create a clear distinction between what is common area and what is mine.

You can hear the wood burning in each of our personal mental stoves. We're driven to invent different ways to carve an existence out of the nonexistent. The greatest inventors of all time didn't possess as much motivation as we now do. What once was a hopeless, barren space is beginning to take on character as each person devotes himself to creating comfort. This "comfort" is not primarily physical. The need to be mentally comfortable is greater.

I'm perusing the tent in an effort to obtain any helpful hints for constructing a life out of my dead space. I have acquired a small remnant of a rug to be placed by my cot. This is so my feet hit something other than sand in the morning. I also just completed making a bookshelf/table out of MRE boxes, a personal clothesline and a collage from photographs of people I wish to stare at each night. This might sound like quite a spread, but I'm able to reach all of it lying flat on my back.

These concoctions are in no way meant to take away the pain of our reality. We build these things in an effort to believe that what we suffer could be worse.

Tomorrow's quote: "When it comes to changes, people only like those they make themselves."[9]

When you gotta go, you gotta go—Visiting a makeshift latrine during a winter rainstorm somewhere in Saudi Arabia

Out here, even the simple act of getting a meal is a chore. Meals entail a one-mile round trip across the nothingness. On my way back from chow, I stumbled upon a skeleton of a camel. If a camel can't survive out here, how can anyone expect us to?

December 26, 1990. The next event to look forward to is New Year's. So much for Times Square. Maybe instead of watching the ball drop we can watch each other do the same.

Saddam just informed the allied forces that we have until January 1, 1991 to pull out of the Middle East. Who the hell does he think he is! He ruined our Christmas, we're not about to let him mess up our grand plan for New Year's! We're not children who run away with the first threat. Besides, we told him to pull out first!

This adjustment is tough for all of us. When I was a Boy Scout, a few days in the woods and I was ready for home. Everyone is trying to accept the situation, but many, like me, are finding it impossible. If this is not Hell, it is the closest I ever wish to get!

Despite the lingering stuffiness in our minds, the air in the tent is light and spirited. Everyone is looking for fun. We pray for moments in which we can lose ourselves. Such moments are rare, worth every cent they pay us to be here. We want to break the chains that bind us to our fears, to abandon ourselves to folly. Tonight is turning into just such a jailbreak. It has taken a while, but everyone has begun to realize that cooperation is better than confrontation. This new attitude materialized when a single soldier cleared the air with a humorous story of how his sister got out of a speeding ticket. The police stopped her and a friend in their car. As the officer approached the car, the girls began rattling on about being chased by another car. They told the officer that they were afraid of the people in that car and that they were attempting to shake them by speeding. Then an innocent car went by, and the girls shouted, "There they go, that's them." The officer sped off, leaving the girls scot-free.

That little story started a comical snowball down a very steep hill. People have been pouring into our tent to share every single joke they know or might have heard. A sergeant came to inform us that we were being too loud. He then realized that the force steering us was bigger than the one that brought us here. Each person who takes the stand to share a joke is a professional comedian. His job is to entertain us until the next act takes the stand. If someone tells a really good joke, he is forced to repeat it. The energy level in this tent is that of a real comedy club. The only thing missing is the drinks.

My favorite joke of the evening: There was an old man who lived in a small town. For many years, he had been an active deacon in the local church. Finally, he decided to leave that up to the young folks. Then he decided to attend when he heard that they were reckoning to spend some money. At the meeting, one of the young members stood up and said "I move that we buy a chandelier for the church." Another seconded "that there motion." The old man stood and said, "Wait one darn minute. I have nothing against progress, but two things concern me. The first being that I don't think there is anyone here that knows how to play it. But what concern me the most is, that we don't need a chandelier as much as we need lights in the church!"

It is late. Joke night has left us exhausted. The comedians have fallen asleep, but not before setting another club date.

We were taken from our separate worlds and placed in this ghetto. It was a shock at first, but it's different now. It has come down to the essentials like cleaning the stove, cleaning the heater, getting the gas, making sure that there's water and food in the tent. We've become a family. It has reached the point that someone will say, "Honey did you clean the stove?" and another will reply, "Do I have to do everything? What do you do all day when I'm at work? You're letting my house go to shit."

We've grown to accept that we all live in the same house. We've begun to watch out for each other. If someone comes in and demands to see someone, one of the others immediately goes on the attack: "Why? What do you want him for?" If that person is wanted for something unpleasant, we reply, "He's busy, get someone else." One outsider came in and demanded to know why one of us had a whole case of water beside his cot, when each person was supposed to have only two bottles. We answered, "It's for everyone in our tent. All the bottles are by his cot because he has the room for them. There are eleven of us in here and only twelve bottles in a case. Bring us another case!"

Each of us has someone in the tent we enjoy picking on, though in a loving way. We also defend that person when an outsider decides to join in. "Stay away from my brother," we'll say, or, "That's my cousin you're messing with!" We defend what we previously denied—each other's rights. Each person has adopted another as his brother. Every one of us has something that we need from another. Those needs range from caring, support and guidance to equipment, batteries, cassette tapes and simple companionship.

I haven't committed to any one person. It seems as though everyone comes to me for whatever they can't get from their brothers. They expect me to provide the missing element. I like it at times. It makes me a kind of spiritual father, which I've been called by some. When we first moved in, everybody had a person or two that they thought could never be their friends. Now, they're not only friends, they're family! If I was told I had a chance to move to another tent with more room, I wouldn't go. I like it here. This place has a security and a sense of humor that no other tent has. It's special. We're finding enjoyment among ourselves. Nobody is helping us. If anything, others are trying to keep us down, because we took the bad and made it good. What is a family for anyway? It's to help those who need it the most. And we all need help—badly!

In addition to our adopted brothers, some of us have adopted fathers. Most of the people here are young, new soldiers who have no knowledge of how to survive a war. Then there are the Veterans. These people have been to war. This situation is different, but they have steadier hands. Most of these fathers have been more than open about sharing their steadiness. For that alone, they are invaluable.

December 27, 1990. I'm coming down with a cold. Even though we're in a desert, it's cold during the day and freezing at night. The trucks have returned to work on the big hole. It's looking more like a swimming pool every day.

We can still find humor in things to safeguard ourselves from the reality of war, but our protection is diminishing against a stronger opponent—boredom.

After last night's comedy marathon, most have settled for relaxing this evening. Almost everyone is listening to Walkmans, reading, writing letters or sleeping.

There's a small beam of light piercing through a tiny hole at the top of the tent, illuminating the particles of dust in its way. This warm, almost spiritual beam of light lands about three inches from my hand.

Every morning in this desert reminds me that there will be many more to follow.

I fear the possibility of going crazy out here. If I do escape this place with my life, I hope my sanity will accompany me.

Tomorrow's quote: "What is a thousand years? Time is short for one who thinks, endless for one who yearns."[10]

Every morning, I awake confronting my death bed.

The only way I'll believe that this is not where I'll die is when I find myself alive—somewhere else!

December 28, 1990. It is so damn cold here. The air warms up a tad in the afternoon. But no sooner do you peel off a layer of clothing than you have to put it back on.

After being here slightly more than a week, it's amazing and educational to see how people have already begun to change—and not just in their daily lives. I'm talking about the way they think or relate to being here, how they feel about everything around them. When we were in Germany, everybody had an exact and different opinion. Now we all have just one: Let's do what we have to do and get the hell out of here. This is an equal-opportunity opinion, held without regard to rank, race or religion.

Most of us have yet to get mail from family and friends, but everyone has a letter or two from somebody we don't know.

December 29, 1990. The day's events have been temporarily halted as a side show has entered our area. They came from across the horizon, coming closer and closer until it was obvious that more than 400 camels were going to trot directly through our camp. Shovels and sand bags were replaced with Instamatics and video cameras, and every one of us had the same thought simultaneously: "The people back home will never believe this."

Since I've been here, I've found myself taking pride in small things—a well-dug fox-hole, an eventless shift of guard duty. I actually enjoy waking up each morning and noticing that I'm still sane. Listening closely one could hear me sing as I turn an MRE into a culinary treat. Maybe I've snapped. Somebody get me out of here before I begin to enjoy this!

Life can give you a jolt sometimes. I'm in a truck riding across the contourless desert on my way back from a Saudi supermarket, listening to the Beastie Boys on my Walkman. The ride has been surreal. We drove over, under and across nothing to pop up at an urban oasis. The place has condos, grass trees and civilian cars. If you drive two miles in any direction you're back in the void. It's also strange to see so many Arabs driving huge American cars—Cadillacs, Fords, Buicks—out in the desert. Why would anyone want a Cadillac for cruising sand?

Now we're driving 100 miles across this wasteland in search of a small military speck. The proverbial needle in a haystack can't begin to compare. And we'll be searching in darkness, without headlights to help us. It's called tactical blackout. It's supposed to prevent the enemy from calculating how many people or vehicles we have. Presumably, only the allies are smart enough to wait until daylight and count at their leisure.

We got back safely. I'm not sure how. I fell asleep expecting to wake up in Egypt.

I was just thinking about this long black object beside me. We've been told it's an M16 rifle. As I look at it and realize what it's intended for, I'm shocked. Until this realization, it was just an object, another piece of Army equipment that I was forced to schlepp around. I never saw it for its intended purpose: Murder!

It is neither easy to accept or to admit, but the quickest way out of this place is for someone to start a war.

Hoping for mail has become a full-time obsession. The desire to receive personal mail is strong. I can feel it in my bones. I need words of encouragement from people I deeply care for. I need to hear that I have not been forgotten, written off or, even worse, presumed dead.

Last night I was listening to my Walkman, the music was the Nutcracker Suite. It's interesting that when musical instruments are played perfectly, they no longer make simple notes or sounds. They become visually animated images, entities. They dance through the imaginations of those who let them.

Once again, all the occupants of our tent are present. Every time this happens, it's a family reunion. Each of us is taking time to hear another's experience. We all have different jobs, and at day's end we share our gossip. It helps us try to figure out what will happen to us. The Army seems uninterested in telling us, so we piece it together ourselves.

Private T has entered the tent to inform us that guards are now being issued live rounds and that his weapon is loaded. Somehow the thrill of knowing that we'll finally be able to defend ourselves has been overtaken by the realization that we can kill. I'm not sure I trust everyone in our unit with the power to take a life. I truly love these guys, but let them earn my trust first.

December 31, 1990. Good morning old life, get ready for the new year. I hope it delivers peace to the world, because the world is sure to suffer under its current regime. Outrage!

Horseplay—This was a friendly wrestling match. But as tensions mounted, such tussles often turned ugly

I can smell action in the air. Right after New Year's, a few crucial players are to move forward to observe and practice something. This is no time for practice! Hey guys, this is the World Series!

For reasons unknown to me, today has become a singing day. Everyone seems to be happily singing something. Why? Have we been told we are going home tomorrow? Has someone forgotten to inform little old me? I walked into the tent to find myself a part of an audience admiring a trio of bellowing soldiers. What's going on? There are two reasons that this bothers me: First, I can't sing; second, even if I could sing, I don't feel like it today.

We must be on another planet. There is no way that Earth, which holds so much beauty, can possess a land with absolutely none.

As we approach the celebration hour, I notice that the moon is so bright it's casting shadows in our camp. We're just minutes from midnight, and I write once again from guard duty. What a way to bring in the New Year!

Well, it's 1991. I turned to my guard partner and delivered a sincere New Year's greeting. He replied by shouting, "Shut the fuck up! Spend your happiness on people who care, if you can find any." I returned to the tent looking for at least one person who would receive my greeting. I wanted to receive one in return. When I got to the tent, everybody was asleep. When was the last time any of these people spent New Year's Eve in bed?

January 1, 1991. The boredom has reached new levels. For fun, the officers have started a mustache-growing competition. The one who leaves the desert with the fullest growth wins. That is excitement!

Like most democracies, we're having a bitch session today. These sessions always begin with good intentions and end up looking like kindergarten at recess.
One can feel the tempers shorten around here.

I just wrote a letter to an ex-girlfriend. At times we all write overzealous letters. We have so many emotions, thoughts, fears. Whenever we sit down to write a calm peaceful letter, these emotions can come pouring out as if the pen had a mind of its own. When we're finished, we feel lighter, so we mail it. Sorry, but that's the truth. We don't really mean all of that stuff.

The thought of being in the middle of nowhere with hundreds of others all having live rounds is scary—though not as terrifying as being without them.

I wish that books could hop from their shelves land in the laps of those who need them. Books should be human. Libraries would be like singles bars. Books would be able to approach those who seem in need. Some small talk would be exchanged, a smile and a drink, then the two of them would go home together. That's silly you say? Well, what is a book but something that sits around waiting to be "picked up"? Books are like most humans, more than willing to share what is between their covers.

We have all grown accustomed to our laziness. We get enraged at the slightest interruption of it.

The darkness tonight is so dense that people are tripping over everything. The wind of war blows by our tent leaving the aroma of fear to waft in aimlessly.

Tomorrow's quote comes from Dorothy Parker: "You can lead a whore to culture, but you can't make her think."

I try to position myself inside this tent, but I will always be outside.

The night is so dark and full of stars, it's like being in a planetarium.

I have written every single person I care to, and a few I didn't. Hopefully, a letter written means a letter received.

January 3, 1991. One of the soldiers in our tent has begun to show a dependency on Actifed.

January 5, 1991. The soldier with the Actifed addiction said, "It's great that you're all talking about me. You'll remember me forever. But by doing this you're making me the main character here. In all the movies I've seen about wars, the main character gets killed, so cut this shit out!"

I have begun to notice that whenever I'm engrossed in writing or sketching, I forget where I am. I get lost in my own creative flow. I wish I could stay in my imagination until this is all over.

We have been receiving news of unrest on the Iraqi side. We heard that an Iraqi helicopter flew across the border to surrender. The soldiers supposedly said that Saddam is not telling them that we're out here and that they have nothing to fear. How can they miss us? We are the 500,000 people on the other end of their telescopes. Hey guys, that's us, the ones in the green with the big guns!

The longer I'm here, the more I'm getting used to it. For that reason alone, my hatred for the army increases each day.

Remember your teens? You had a big date coming up, and you could feel the jitters mounting as you developed a zit. At times you would feel the growth coming on a whole week before it appeared on your face. Well that's how we all feel—but the blemish is a whole lot bigger than a pimple.

I have just finished flipping through my journal. I noticed that we were moving along at a nice pace until recently. The beginning entries were like a runaway tire racing down a hill. Lately the tire has been rolling uphill with nothing behind it. We're stagnant, ready to stop and roll backward. We all worked so hard to keep up our spirits in the presence of opposing forces. We're now feeling the gravity.

Flan, who is one of my tentmates, just shared a poem with me. I'm constantly amazed to find such minds hidden behind military camouflage. Does anyone have any idea of the human spirits that are in danger of being extinguished? There should be a screening process. The Army surely doesn't know how to use people's true abilities properly. It's like using a Jaguar in a demolition derby or wearing a tuxedo to sweep chimneys.

January 8, 1991. We have been put on alert, because we've passed the deadline given by Saddam. All is quiet, but no one can remain still. We've also received news that Saddam's air force has been showing a lot of activity. Tomorrow, we'll begin air-raid drills. The guards' weapons are locked and loaded, and tensions are as high as our combined blood pressures. I feel the upcoming pain the way an old, arthritic woman feels the next day's rain in her bones.

My current mood is new to me. I have never encountered anything like it before. It's more than fear of death. It's like the end is here—though it doesn't know what I look like, and it is searching for me. I have only one wish if I am to die, that is simply to have one more day than my canceled life would allow.

January 9, 1991. The threat is thickening as the two cooks—Saddam and George Bush—stir the pot. It's going to be a long evening. We were told to sleep in full uniform. Everyone in the tent has crawled inside himself. Some quietly lift weights, read and listen to music. Others stare into the thickened air. We can no longer hear last night's laughter.

We're about to meet Man's absolute challenge. I am frightened for my life. I have smoked more cigarettes in this desert than all my years of smoking combined.

January 10, 1991. We've had two fire drills in the past twenty-four hours. There are large foxholes directly in front and behind each tent. When a fire drill is called everyone runs to the nearest hole and does a half-flip with a twist to safety.

Saddam has moved his air force into the ready position. We are at full alert and were told to expect an attack at 0500.

The tent is busy. People are packing and scattering their belongings, searching for the things they'll need in case of attack. Every one of us is taking time to write what may be our last letters to those we love. I am so scared it hurts. I couldn't sleep with twenty Quaaludes in me.

The following segment is directed to my parents, friends, and especially to those who are extra close to me:

I have lived a much shorter time than I wish to live. The memories you have planted in my head helped me through my life, more than you could possibly realize. I love all of you even if I am never capable of telling you. At this moment, you are Priority One in my mind. It's difficult to be specific right now. All of my thoughts are wrestling for attention. All I am able to do is cry a lot and write very little. I will swear to whatever god really exists: Let me endure, and I will do better in the future. I promise never to purposely place myself in a position that endangers my life and calls for such desperation. I only wish that I had received mail from all those I wrote to, for reading your thoughts would mean so much. It's hard to sum up my life and my thanks in a few words or metaphors. None come to mind anyway. I only hope that what I have completed in life and the writings in this book can at least begin to express who I am—or was.

I'm now on a sleep cycle. Most are on guard through the night. We now take turns sleeping in the peace from the light of day, because we guard in the terror of the darkness.

There is no way I can sleep knowing that my death could be so near. I feel sick to my stomach. I can only sit still, thinking of everything and nothing at the same time.

My friend Flan just told me that he received another letter addressed to Any Soldier. He wants to write back and address it from Not Just Any Soldier!

January 11, 1991. It looks like the other side is now The Boy Who Cried Wolf.

This morning in the cold, I sat alone in a hole for seven hours. That's what I call time spent with yourself! The sun has come up, letting us all relax. I'm now tucked away in my sleeping bag, ready to hibernate till the dark covers us again.

Well, as usual my plans for rest were not in sync with the army's plans for me. I'm sitting in the sand prying my eyes open near two barrels of burning shit. I've had two hours of sleep in forty-eight. The smell of the burning feces is making me want to kill someone, though the heat is keeping me warm and close. There are rules for the proper burning of shit. You have to use one part gasoline and one part diesel fuel. Then you must risk life and limb to ignite the mixture, following up with almost three hours of stirring, mixing, adding and vomiting. Note: It burns more effectively if you are able to drain the urine from the barrel before burning, though this is not a preferred method.

That night we ran for our foxholes, and sat for hours in pure fright, is still causing much pain and confusion. I'm no longer secure in my ability to handle what lies ahead. I question my own strength and stability.

It's time once again to try to sleep. There was no mail for me—again. Mail to a soldier in Desert Shield is like sex to a man in a singles bar.

January 12, 1991. Yesterday was another wolf cry, but the aroma of war still lingers. Everyone knows it's coming. I believe we'll win. America will go to any length to ensure that they don't lose two big ones in a row. They'll rejoice over the victory and deny all inhuman acts attributed to it.

"Youth is the first victim of war; the first fruit of peace. It takes twenty years or more of peace to make a man: only twenty seconds of war to destroy him."[11]

When and if I live through this I will take time and care to plan the rest of my life. It's much more important to me—and others—than I had previously thought. I want to plan for it because I know I can't do things as I did before. To show where my previous actions got me, I pick up some sand and let it fall through my fingers.

Medical brothers and sister—Cummings, Fortune, Elmer; representing nearly half of HHB Divarty's medical unit of seven

54

Up to this point my job has been making maps and charts of the war's progress and plans. Now I'm a medic again. The change forced itself on me during an exercise in chemical protection. We all walk around with protective masks on our hips. With the first sign of chemical warfare, we are to put on these masks immediately. I have no problem with that part—I am all for saving myself—but I have extreme reservations about the unmasking procedures. The person who takes his or her mask off first is a guinea pig, testing the air for everyone else. We have millions of dollars worth of equipment to test everything we do, but this process is left to trial and error. But what I really object to is the way this person is chosen: Anyone who's job is considered nonessential is eligible. I don't know any human being who is nonessential enough to die for any other, simply because someone tells him his job isn't important. I mention this because I was just told that I am nonessential by someone who was not open to philosophical debate on the subject.

So it's back to being a medic, which should let me breathe again. One of the medics broke his arm in a fire drill. It was dark, the alarm was sounded, he ran for his life—and almost ended it when he plummeted into an eight-foot foxhole. This leaves an opening for a medic, and considering how close we are to being shot at, I am sure they wouldn't mind a replacement.

Once again, it's raining. It rains here more than it does in Northern Europe, though nothing grows. It feels more like Germany than one would expect in a desert. I can't wait till this place is a distant memory!

We've heard that Saddam will strike on or about January 14 at 3:00 A.M. That is only nine hours and forty-five minutes from now.

As I wrote that last passage I stopped to observe my tentmates. They've all gone mad, carrying on as if the war is over. Why? The war is obviously not over. It's about to begin. I see no call for such behavior, though I envy them as they dance and shout on the edge of the abyss. It takes a truly brave or oblivious person to act this way. Why can't I participate? Do I lack their courage, or do I possess something they lack? I can't figure it out, though I'd rather feel any other way than I do right now. Victory—not much of a substitute for lost lives. In a war there are only losers. Everyone suffers, but the dead get stuck with the tab.

I'm nervous as hell. We are packing and preparing. We have to be ready, even when the boy only cries Wolf.

An alarm just sounded. Soldiers are pouring out of the door and jumping out of their skins and into foxholes and guard posts, which I must do as well. It is going to be a long night!

I've grown beyond fear. I've crossed into a frightful dimension that words cannot describe.

"What a country calls its vital…interests are not things that help its people live, but things that help it make war. Petroleum is a more likely cause of international conflict than wheat."[12]

January 14, 1991. We were stood up again. That's OK. I don't mind a bit. I have to keep showing up anyway.

As I walked into the tent it appeared—and still appears to me—to be another tent. This place can't be mine, for mine is always a joyous place. This place feels strange, mysterious, evil. I don't like it at all.

I'm now located at the main camp as a medic. Everything is new—job, tent, my tentmates, boss, frame of mind—everything. I'm now essential. I normally don't care what other people think, but in this case, I need the Army to think exactly as I do. If I want better odds of surviving, I need them to think I'm important.

My living quarters are actually in the TMC (Troop Medical Clinic), along with five others. I feel a bit more comfortable here. If anything happens, I'll be able to react in a way that could do some good. I'd be helping to save a life rather than drawing a map.

I just returned from guard duty, where my partner and I spent the whole two hours trying to recall the password. On my way back I had stopped by the female tent to pick up a poetry book from one of the soldiers there. Everyone in her tent was asleep. We stood on the so-called porch, exchanged a few whispered words and smiles in the dark, then I turned and went to my tent. I have no feelings for this woman, but standing there with the moonlight and talking of poetry reminded me of many evenings in college. It was a warm feeling.

It's late now. Earlier, when I returned from guard duty the sergeant who is my boss came to me and we had a talk. We discovered we both lived in Columbus, Ohio at the same time. We even knew some of the same people and places. It was great to talk with someone about familiar topics. We also shared a drink. His wife had sent him plastic martini glasses, olives, cocktail onions, and The New York Times. Only the gin was missing.

January 15, 1991. I awoke to the smell of breakfast, a good string of oldies on the radio and stimulating conversation. I like my new home already.

Today is Saddam's deadline for pulling out of Kuwait. War will start any time now. The skies have been full of planes lately. Something is afoot.

Once again, it's time for darkness to creep over us. We hold our breath and hide from the fear within us so that we can function. We sit in dark, cold, damp holes, speculating on how our world is about to change.

This is all so strange to me. How can I be in such danger? I long for a chance to start over.

How will this all end? What will be left of me? I fear losing. Most of all, I fear myself.

January 16, 1991. Somebody needs to do something! The waiting and anticipation are becoming unbearable.

Tomorrow I have KP, which is slave work. One cleans and scrapes the pots that the cooks burn and scar.

Once again, as if we weren't already on the edge of our seats, we received more threatening news. The "ball game" will begin any day now. The attitudes around here have switched from antiwar to pro-war, for the sooner the game begins, the sooner it's over—and the sooner we can head to the locker room.

PART FIVE

Storm—A Fitting Title

January 17, 1991. Shit! We're at war! The air raid started while we slept. We had a hunch something was about to happen—but not now! I thought someone would warn us, give us twenty-four hours' notice. Nothing! While we slept, war lurked in the darkness.

We learned of it when a female sergeant entered our tent, wearing her protective mask and chemical suit. "Fellas, fellas," she whispered. "Gas!" The war started as if it were trying not to wake us. But we got the message. As if on fire, we stumbled out of bed, scraped up our equipment and headed for our guard posts. Then nothing. All was quiet. Another false alarm, I thought.

We waited in the darkness of early morning and early war—nervous, scared, unsure of what was to follow, and not wishing to find out. This morning's sunrise seemed to be handicapped. The colors were there, but the beauty was gone.

After the sunrise, everyone ran to a radio to hear for themselves that it was really true. Nobody wanted to believe it, and no one ate breakfast. The news kept repeating the same reports over and over, as if to convince the nonbelievers, "It's no longer Desert Shield." They're calling the war Desert Storm. How fitting. I've been using that metaphor since I began this journal.

But not even war can halt KP. I'm on a break listening to CNN tell me things I don't want to know. I'm trying to relax and forget about the slavish chores I just completed, and

By the dawn's early light—For the U.S. troops, such artillery barrages meant spectacular light shows; for the Iraqis at the other end, they meant death

61

all those I have yet to do. All I can think about is the reality of the war. The radio is not helping. It's one thing to be here and see all that's happening around me; it's quite another to hear what's happening out in the world—especially when it makes bad news worse. This whole war thing is a political balancing act.

It's evening again. I've finished KP, and it's time to fall into a deep sleep. Maybe I'll awake to peace. Fat chance!

Since we're not on the front lines, there is no evidence of actually being in war—yet. If the war doesn't come to us, though, I'm afraid we'll go to it. My initial reaction this morning was to do what everyone else was doing. I have no idea what else to do, except to write down what was happening.

January 18, 1991. This morning feels different from any other, for we awoke to the certain knowledge of war. We slept knowing what awaits us on the other side of our dreams—our nightmares.

There has been twenty-four-hour bombing of Bagdad, and Israel has been attacked by Iraq. Violence is escalating every minute. I feel as though we're teetering on the edge of World War III!

I feel choked. I can't breathe. The air is getting thinner by the minute, as though the war is pulling the very oxygen out of it.

In the military there is a crucial piece of equipment known as a MOPP suit. We all have them; we all need them. The acronym isn't important. What is important is that the suits are essential to our survival in a chemical attack. Each of us has two of them. This morning almost everyone in the Allied force broke the seals on one of their precious suits, thus rendering them useless in future attacks. We put them on and stood in the pouring rain on Stand To. There was no attack.

Why did we do it? Apparently a radio news report said that there was a possibility of chemicals in the Scuds that hit Israel, which is very far away from any of us. Someone in the military must have heard this and told the entire army to go to full protection levels.

Don't eat the Chicken a la King—MREs (Meal Ready Eats) being unloaded for GI consumption—and contempt

Brilliant, huh? Now because of this anonymous genius, we have only one suit apiece, and are due to enter Iraq soon. We were also told to hang onto the ruined suits. Maybe they're planning a garage sale. Does anybody want to buy 500,000 ugly green army suits that don't work?

We must not be on the mailman's route, for we've had little or no mail. We don't have a dog, so what the hell is the problem? Everyone in the military has a job and somewhere out there are those who are supposed to deliver the mail—though God knows where they are; they're certainly not in these parts. I haven't received even one letter from anyone to whom I wrote, though I have received a couple from those to whom I didn't. It's hard to find things to write to people anymore. I've exhausted the usual things that people in a war write to those who aren't. I need to get letters so I can answer the questions they carry.

Once more, the act of eating something has developed into a need. I've ignored it far too long, but both my choices are unappetizing. Let's examine them. I can go to that mobile stomachache known as the mess hall, or I can eat my one-millionth MRE. If you are what you eat, I should be as fresh twenty years from now as I am today. The mobile kitchen, by contrast, offers a mandatory one-course meal guaranteed to be as stale today as it was when they tried to serve it last week.

It's time I described MREs in detail. They come twelve in a box, each box containing the same assortment of twelve different meals. Each of these "meals," in turn, allegedly contains all one needs for nutritious eating. Each certainly contains all one needs to be quite ill. Most of us can only stomach two or three of the twelve, which means that day after day we eat the same bad food. There's a saying; if you add a little seasoning, heat them up, and consume them with enough bread, they still taste like shit.

The selections on the menu include turkey and ham loaf (that's one meal), a freeze-dried beef or pork patty with beans, omelette with ham (which resembles Silly Putty and tastes worse), turkey diced with gravy, and my favorite, meatball beef and rice. (Its official name raises a question: If this meal has beef and rice in it, what are the meatballs made from?) In addition to the delicious main courses, MREs also come with desserts such as baby apple sauce, freeze-dried fruit mix, or, worst of all, fruit cake. If you are lucky enough to be the one trillionth customer you may get a five-year-old bag of M&Ms (far too late to enter the contest on the back of the package).

There are other selections, but none is as mysterious as the most evil MRE of all. Almost no one can get past its label: Chicken a la King. You'll find it in every otherwise empty MRE box in the world. Most of us would kill to avoid it. Words can't describe how vile it is, though if you're curious, you could go to your nearest Army-Navy store and experience one for yourself. I will not be responsible for your hospital bill.

Now that I've finished writing this section, I think I'll have a box of Oreos and call it dinner. Sorry, Mom. I wish you could send me all those vegetables I never ate.

January 19, 1991. I am well-rested, but I feel tired, drained, like I am giving blood—which in a way I am, though it's not voluntary.

I hope Saddam doesn't succeed in turning this into a Holy War. It seems to me that when he was little, he must have been the kid on the block that never played fair.

I got another letter from a stranger. This person says he doesn't know what to write about. I like this, for most wish us well and tell us that they are praying for us. Those are nice thoughts, but these people don't even know us. They're writing what they think we'd like to hear. I'd rather hear from someone with his own thoughts, even if he has trouble expressing them.

The air attack has been going on for two days. The radio has finally stopped broadcasting the same news twenty-four hours a day and has resumed playing music. What really bothers me is that CNN constantly shows footage of the bombing, accompanied by comments such as, "Ooh look at that," or "As you can see." We can't see! We are listening to a damn radio!

Ah, I just returned from using the telephones. I feel better now that I was able to talk to my family and a few friends. The ordeal involved getting there was hell. I drove a large truck full of people about 30 miles across the desert. No physical damage was reported, though I was questioned about my driving abilities. (That's OK, I don't even have a license.) We all stepped down from the truck and directly into a line. It's not that we parked anywhere near the actual phones; the line was about a mile long and lead to a large white circus tent that housed about 100 telephones. We waited an hour and a half before I could see the phones, then two more hours before I touched one. It took a few minutes, but I composed myself enough to recall how to dial. I first called my parents. After they woke up, we talked for the allotted twenty minutes, then I got back in line to repeat the process. My parents told me that all my relatives, even those I hardly know, are going to write and send food. Next I talked to a friend from college. She said that everyone in the States is going crazy; they've canceled school for a couple of days so people can watch the news. She also said that the war footage is making everyone very worried. I said that's nice, I won't be able to sleep knowing that people who are safely in the States are worried.

I just bought a T-shirt that says "Hard Rock Cafe, Baghdad, Opening Soon."

Yes, the war is going on, people are dying by the thousands, cities are being leveled, and I will be going into Iraq in a week or two, but for now we carry on as if the war never started.

I never thought I'd be tired of sodas and junk food, but I am. Someone can offer me a Pepsi or some cookies and I'll shy away as if it was liver.

Something else unique to this place: the Paperbacks from Hell. They're everywhere. Soldiers brought them along, and they're being shipped here in great numbers. Every tent has a huge stack. The floor of every truck is lined with them. Most of them are mysteries or soft-porn romance. (Some are not that soft.) But there are also books on military topics, such as Vietnam or WWII. The last thing I'd want to read in this place would be a war book.

Just when boredom was reaching record highs, our surroundings have supplied us with a new sport: mouse-killing. We've been told that the mice here carry numerous unpleasant diseases. The slaughter started this morning when a guy in my tent awoke to find that the precious headset to his Walkman had been surgically removed by one of the creatures. Now we stalk them with knives attached to broom handles, baseball bats, and an assortment of other deadly instruments. We really try to harm the little varmints, but they're not only faster than we are, they're smarter as well. Once in a while we get lucky and find one asleep on the job.

The mailman just came. The mailman just left. Nothing!

I've stopped the quote of the day out of lack of interest from anyone besides me.

Preflight check—A technician prepares a battery of surface-to-air missiles during the division's rapid sweep through Iraq

Once in a while someone will ask me what it is; I just blurt out an old one. They don't know the difference.

All around us, day and evening, I can hear the sounds of exploding rounds, missiles, and artillery shells. All the surrounding units are practicing for the war, like the Olympic trials. I hope we get the gold!

The nights here bring on a certain feeling. I haven't yet figured out exactly what it is or what it means, but there is definitely something in the night air. I can feel it as clear as rain on my head. Last night I strolled about the camp, and with every step that landed on the sand in front of me I heard musical notes. I felt emotions I never felt before. With each step I took, with each star I noticed, with every second that crawled by, I was introduced to these emotions and sounds. In the lonely silence, I have made friends and created good feelings within me. At times like these, I feel that I can survive this place.

Oh, I do love it here! This morning on guard, we endured rain and hail. Sitting in the middle of a desert absorbing bullets of ice, we sat and sat and sat. One would ask why we didn't seek shelter. The answer is that we were told to stay put! When the storm subsided and I gained enough courage to raise my head, I saw that my sergeant and I were all alone. Everyone else had fled. Typical!

As we sat helpless in the hail, Israel endured another Scud attack. Iraq sent ten Scuds, but the Patriot missiles destroyed nine. I love those damn Patriot missiles.

Since the war has began, the hours seem to fly by, though the days crawl along.

I'm watching the flaps that make the door to this tent. They're wrestling in the wind. First they gently brush each other, rubbing as if romantically involved. They sway to and fro sharing their texture with each other, then as the air grows more violent, they begin to shove at one another as if playing King of the Tent. This escalates into an abusive brawl. Each flap takes its turn at being the aggressor, while the other plays victim. Then they're suddenly closed and calm, brushing ever so lightly together, as if in a courtship. They lie innocent and peaceful only until the air engages them once again, and the cycle of fighting and making up resumes.

My God! I need some other kind of entertainment than staring at the mating rituals of wind-blown fabric! Surely there is something better to do. Maybe I could watch mice trying to break into an MRE, or if I am really hard up, I can listen to my stomach recite "We Are The World."

The time has come to shed light on the dark and medieval rituals of bathing and relieving oneself in the desert. First bathing: We have two choices—three, really, though the third lies in ignoring the other two. One option is to venture to what we laughingly call the shower. It's a wooden box with rusty metal container on top that holds unclean water full of rust, sand and other unidentified stuff. If this is your means of cleansing, you must dig deep into yourself to find whatever it takes to withstand freezing water pouring on you in trickles, in winter weather, with a cold desert wind blowing air and sand on you the whole time. After you've been brought back to life and remember how to breathe, you must venture back across the desert to your tent. When you arrive, you notice two things: First, you're dirtier than you were when you left; second, everyone else has stayed in the tent to exercise Option Two.

This is also known as the "whore's bath," which I guess gets its name from the days when prostitutes did it between customers. The process requires a few important elements: a large plastic bowl of hot water, a wash cloth, cleansing accessories, your naked body and perfect timing. (Someone is bound to enter when you're most vulnerable.) Then and only then do you feel as bad as you look when approaching the sensitive areas of your body, feeling as though you're auditioning for a sleazy movie.

With Option Two, you can remain semi-clean until morning—unless you feel the urge to relieve yourself. Now we're in forbidden territory. If anyone ever reads this, I'm sure to turn a head or two. "No, not me," they'll say. "I never did that." Don't believe them. If they were here in this desert, they did it.

To keep things as respectable as possible, I'll refer to the functions No. 1 and No. 2. Depending on your garment status, you have choices here as well. If you're a man and have to do No. 1, all you have to do is put on your uniform and your war paraphernalia, which takes about five minutes. Then you run across the camp to relieve yourself in a small tube stuck in the ground. If you're a woman, you either go to the women's latrine, or you can opt for the Second Method. This option is a product of urgency, convenience, laziness and all of the above. All you need is an empty water bottle. (If you're a woman you also need a knife to increase the size of the opening.) But you have to be prepared to live with the stuff. Besides seeing paperback books and Walkmans in every tent, we also see every shade of urine beside each cot. Truly lazy people have more than one bottle. This is a problem only when you drink the MRE Kool-Aid flavor of orange.

That leaves No. 2, a normally simple process that the desert has transformed into a dreaded chore. It begins in the tent as you sit comfortably on your cot. The less clothing you have on the more susceptible you are to the urge. Any time you leave your tent, you must be wearing the proper uniform and equipment. The items that make up this burden are protective mask, utility belt with a few pounds of ammunition attached, helmet, weapon and a rucksack containing an assortment of things that may save your life if the camp is attacked while you're relieving yourself. After loading all this equipment on, there is a short walk to the latrine, where you take it all off to do your business. The latrines here are identical to the makeshift contraptions at the Chutzpah Filling Station. If luck is on your side, you'll be alone. If not, you'll be sharing the box with three other people. There you'll be trapped, sitting close enough for your legs to touch, relieving yourselves, trying to ignore each other. After the awkwardness of wiping yourself, you then get dressed again and return to your tent, wishing that you had never left. By the way, night-time visits have their own elements of danger, since you can't see where you're sitting or what you're sitting in.

I tend to dwell on the rudiments of desert life. This is because on days like this, when nothing is happening, these rudiments stick up like gigantic speed bumps. We're reminded of the difficulties of desert living every day.

We just had a pep talk from our commander. It wasn't really a going-to-war sermon. It was more like a game of Capture the Flag. We're not going to play touch football, unless it counts by touching every person that you killed first!

Nobody knows for sure when we'll move forward. I feel a small wave of depression washing away my optimism.

Whenever I find myself slipping into a mood that can harm me, I dive into my past. Sometimes I find myself in the past without remembering how I got there. I'm happy that my past has been full and rich. I owe my stability to all those who are a part of it.
I have no idea what day it is, and I'm too lazy to ask.

Why is it that my best memories, the ones that give me the most satisfaction, are of

Junk food fix—A soldier returns from the PX, a mobile facility that followed the troops through the desert selling snacks and toiletries

70

the time in my life that ended up putting me in this hell? Those wonderful days of care-lessness and promiscuity were the building blocks for the invisible walls that isolate me here. Yet I use the memories to carry me through. Life is strange!

I have been writing this journal for seven weeks. I've never written so much before. I wonder why. I do know that my diligence in keeping this journal is the sole reason I'm still sane. Whenever I feel lost in fright or confusion, I write. I jot down that which gives me pain and discomfort. Later when I am more at ease I study my fears, evaluate my sin-cerity, and discover a piece of myself I hadn't met yet.

January 22, 1991. Nothing remotely interesting happened at all.

January 23, 1991. A public-affairs officer stopped by our camp this morning. He want-ed people to say hello to their families. I asked if I could read a quote or two, he said yes, but we were never able to decide on one. Every time I presented him with a quote I liked, he shot it down, saying it was too depressing. Then he would offer quotes that I wouldn't be caught dead reciting. He commented that if I couldn't come up with anything happy to say to people in the States, I wouldn't be permitted to say anything at all.

That's just great. We wouldn't want anyone to think we're not enjoying this. These people are driving me nuts! We're living worse than cave men. We're here to fight a war, which means killing and (for some of us) being killed, but we can't have anyone think we're not having the time of our lives.

Israel has been hit again! This makes it the third time. They've been really good sports about it.

"Join the Army, travel to exotic lands, meet exotic people and kill them."

I was talking to my friend Don, I mentioned that I thought it would be interesting if everyone had a harmonica lodged in his mouth. We would all communicate by producing sounds and noises that would resemble music. He said, "I am glad your idea doesn't involve a tuba."

Tuning in—Information was scarce in the desert, especially through official channels. This soldier is listening to the BBC

The weather has been nasty for a few days. Now it has cleared up. Let the bombing commence.

It's a sunny afternoon. I'm sitting outside on our makeshift porch, watching soldiers play baseball to relieve their aggressions. The air is brushing by my recently exposed scalp, thanks to an evil haircut. All day I've been telling people that I'm learning to walk backwards. The ball game is intense. People are attacking it as if it were the World Series. Well, in a way it is—and this release of energy and spirit is more important and will be with them longer than any they've ever seen on television.

The moon must be full, for the spirit of the camp has taken a bizarre turn. People are roaming around talking and fooling with anything and everyone they come across. You'd be surprised at what can be entertaining and even funny when you so desperately need it to be!

There's a lack of material to write about, for once again we are stagnant. We've been in one spot too long. I hate waiting and doing stupid little things to occupy myself, fooling my own mind into believing that time is moving. It isn't.

Again no mail. I know it's out there somewhere. The thought that it's accumulating in a pile, waiting for someone to get off his ass to deliver it, makes me angry.

January 24, 1991. Today I burned shit, burned trash, drove to another unit and received the runaround, and returned to no mail. Typical day.

Earlier I may have mentioned Stand Two. This unique ritual takes place every morning from 5:00 A.M. to 7:00 A.M. Actually it begins at a quarter to five, when our dreams are intruded on by the preparations for this torture. The military name for this is Stand To, which means you stand to confront the enemy at the most vulnerable time—sunup. We changed it because all it means to us is that we have to stand for two hours. The process begins with a phone call on our landline phone or by an unwelcome high-ranking individual impolitely canceling our dreams with the words, "It's that time again!" Loudly! We poke our heads ever so slowly from our sleeping wombs saying, "OK, we know, we know." Then we doze off for another five or ten precious minutes.

Suddenly one brave soul takes the plunge, and the rest of us follow. At glacial speed, we pack on enough clothing to survive the North Pole for a month. By this time we're fifteen minutes late. We're always informed of this by another telephone call or another rude intrusion by the officer. We're quite aware of it but untouched by any sense of urgency. Then we face the cold. Our flashlights are equipped with a red filter that can't illuminate anything. It only gives the darkness a red tint. In this ghostly light, we continue onward—tripping, tumbling and injuring ourselves on everything from tent ropes and stakes to foxholes and trucks. Once we're past these invisible obstacles, we nurse our injuries and spend a few minutes walking in various wrong directions. No matter how many times we approach this stage, we have no idea where we're going. Then, with luck or a little help from friends, we arrive at our designated patch of nothingness.

You see, we have to venture across a mile of sand in the dark to find a certain spot, two feet square. Then begins a bizarre assortment of rituals designed to fill a two-hour wait in the cold, watching nothing but the darkness slip away into the morning. The only semi-enjoyable thing about this is that we see every sunrise every morning without exception. There's also something disturbing about watching the sun rise with a loaded rifle, chemical protection gear and an intent to kill anything that the sun exposes. Somehow, the timeless poetry of the moment has been lost.

Some dig down into the sand; others build it up, protecting themselves from an enemy who stands us up every morning. Then there are those who try to sleep, but are awakened by the snap of their necks as their helmets fall abruptly forward. Groups of friends tend to migrate toward each other, like buzzards around a carcass. Those who stand alone have their own hobbies. They entertain themselves by playing with rocks—throwing them, building with them, kicking, stomping, collecting, or arranging them in any and all ways that rocks can do these things. This morning I chose to walk around in a circle until I had made a deep ring in the ground. I mentioned to those who passed that I'll have ponies tomorrow and will be selling rides.

Finally, Stand Two. We return to our tents, stopping by the mess hall to pick up delicious MREs for breakfast. The scary thing is that Stand To has become routine. We no longer think about it. We just do it every morning before we realize we're awake. We endure it because we have to. I choose to use it as a playground, a kind of proving ground for my sanity. By the way, the direction that we are pointed in as we stand and wait is towards friendly territory. We guard ourselves from other Americans. No one has yet explained that to me!

January 27, 1991. We're in a period of official downtime. We're supposed to relax. How? They must be insane! I'm in a desert, waiting for war and possibly death, and they expect me to relax!

After Stand Two, a bunch of us drove to the telephones. I was able to reach my brother, my parents and my girlfriend in Germany. It's hard to describe how wonderful it is to talk to these people—or anyone actually, anyone who knows me and can talk about things other than this damn war. What angers me is when they tell me of all the great things that they and others have sent in the mail. They ask how I liked them. My answer was that they were great and they will be even better when I get them. Every time I confront my mailless cot I feel like killing a mailman.

One of the guys in my tent just got some bad news. His father is dying. His family sent a Red Cross message three days ago—and even that got lost in the sand. He's now trying to arrange emergency leave to go home and see his father before he dies. I hope the Army can find the heart to grant it.

January 28, 1991. Yesterday, after I returned from using the telephones, I was asked to drive the Chaplain to another unit, so I did. Then I had to drive back alone. Me alone behind a wheel of a truck without a license! I had a ball! I was singing, yelling, carrying on like a lunatic. This gave me an independent feeling, one that is almost impossible to achieve out here. I'm always around other people. There I was alone, with no one else to tell me what to do. I could have driven anywhere, except that I was afraid to get lost or killed, so I drove straight to the camp. But I did it in style, careening across the desert like a raving idiot.

I'm watching soldiers play softball as I pray for mail.

My tentmate is leaving tomorrow to see his father. For his sake, I hope that he can stay there and miss the war. For my sake, I want him to return because I will miss our conversations. Talking with him has been an important part of my days.

Praise the Lord and pass one-liners—The division chaplain, shown here with his desert-camouflage Bible, dispensed equal, very welcome portions of spiritual guidance and high comedy

January 29, 1991. Mail! A package from my girlfriend with edible German goodies and a letter from a dear friend in the States. The items she sent made me feel as if I were back in Germany, though the feeling lasted only a minute.

One of the sergeants in my unit and I have adopted a ritual for mail that seems to work. We press three fingers together, close our eyes and recite a silent prayer to the evil god of the postal service. So far so good.

It's amazing. At times I'll be sitting around unproductively thinking about nothing special and catch myself in my past. I tend to dwell more on what has happened in my life than on what will happen. I guess this is due to not being able to see past the immediate future, which could be "all she wrote!" At times, I hear a very large woman warming up her voice.

Oh my God, hold me back! Sound the alarm! There were two mail deliveries today! What's happening? Did someone forget to be lazy? I received another package, as did others in the tent. We now have enough junk food to last a long while—well, maybe a short while.

I'm very tired, though I wish never to stop thinking. I wonder what it would be like if I could record my thoughts as I slip out of consciousness through slumber and back to consciousness, recording all that occurred from the beginning of a dream till the realization of its being over. What a trek that would be!

I wish to find the words to express how I often feel, though I often feel that there are no words to express my feelings.

For some reason I developed an angry, almost violent attitude while I wrote a letter to a friend. It began with good intentions. As I reached the part about describing my surroundings and how I felt about them, I became enraged. I turned a sweet and beautiful letter into an I-hate-the-world diatribe! Now that the letter is done and hidden in an envelope, I am still angered—not by what I wrote, but why it was written and the fact that it was blurted out involuntarily.

A lot of soldiers are getting in trouble around here, losing rank and having their pay docked. The reasons are stupid but understandable. We all have short fuses. All it takes is for one person's flame to get too close to another's. We've had at least two fights a day. When the time comes to fight the real war, we'll still be recovering from this one.

The following is a list of things that I am sick and tired of: Nothingness, sand, rocks, mud, MREs, the color green, tents, Stand Two, a cold desert, the Army as a whole, NCOs who shouldn't have their rank, privates who think they're captains, water bottles, urinating, darkness, KP, burning shit, shitting in a barrel, being outdoors, trash, sunrise, Walkmans, headphones, my cassette tapes, boots, dust, thinking of women, showering in subzero weather, rats, candy and cookies, writing five letters to a person without receiving one in return, flashlights, camo sleeping bags, having no space to breath, not being able to express myself except in this journal—and listening to other people tell me what they're sick and tired of!

The first thing I'll do when I return to Germany is go to the bank, grab a handful of cash, run to the train station and jump on the first ride to another country—anywhere. I don't care! I just have to get away from all these people as quickly as possible.

January 31, 1991. It's been a long day on KP. I feel like the worn-out sponge I just discarded.

We haven't received mail in two days and were told there will be none for a week or so, because the mail unit is moving a mile from their present location due to rats. Come on! I can't believe that shit.

Tempers are flaring around here as the rumors fly and misinterpreted information gets filtered down to us. Plus we found out that the news received last week (about a few little battles we supposedly won along the border) was nothing but propaganda constructed by the Army to give us the impression that all is well. How good can it be if they have to play games with our heads?

February 1, 1991. I just returned from watching hundreds of people practice firing their rifles. I was there to make sure they didn't shoot each other.

February 2, 1991. Today I walked around with a tape recorder and made a cassette of nonsense to send my parents. I interviewed various characters and had them describe daily life in the desert. This way my parents can have a view other than mine. I had a lot of fun doing it. I also learned a few things. I learned that I was not the only one who has been spending enough thought on our situation to justify independent study credits. The course is Mental Stability. The Army always talks about how we're eligible for college credits from job and life experiences. If this is true, then everyone out here will earn a bachelor's degree in life by the time we leave. I've also learned that the long-term effects of being in the desert are affecting everyone. Even those who have been in war before are finding it hard to deal with the surroundings.

The Chaplain is a unique individual, he reminds me of Father Mulcahy in M*A*S*H, but funnier. He's like a religious stand-up comic. He'll give you a little sermon on life then follow it up with a joke or two. He should be on a stage. A lot of us owe our sanity to this man. It's not the religious help that has made him essential, it's that he's a great human being.

I'm actually getting used to this barbaric way of living. Each day I find myself fighting it less and less.

I just put stitches in a patient's head. I get real satisfaction from the accomplishment of a task like that. It makes me feel essential.

Since I started writing in this journal I haven't missed a twelve-hour period without documenting something. I think that I am afraid to stray away from my journal and written thoughts. My journal and I are like mother and child. If I stray too far I could be lost forever.

February 3, 1991. It's cool and windy today; a small sandstorm is brewing outside. I woke up angry from an afternoon nap. The antics of my tentmates have ceased to be amusing. Every single noise they make sends chills of hatred up my already twisted spine; every shriek of stupidity rattles the bars on my cage. I hope they don't continue to affect me in this way. Opening the cage would be a nightmare! I'm so fed up with everything. I'm ready to pounce!

I've retreated to the far end of the tent. I'm still affected by the adolescence of my tentmates, but their sounds follow me everywhere I go. I'm seated in a foldout chair facing those angry, wind-blown tent flaps. I feel like they look.

How could I have become so lost? Nothing I ever learned prepared me for this. I'm no longer what I was: a young artist with a scholarship, friends and a promising future. I'm a

Waiting for war—Desert Shield was a succession of tense moments such as this

80

soldier, a statistic, with nothing to look forward to but death. I'm trying to get back on the old path, but no one here seems to know the way, and there are no gas stations in sight to ask for directions.

The following is the ending to a letter I just wrote to an old girlfriend. I didn't intend to be so passionate, but it took on a life of its own. Now that it lives, I can't change it:

"I long to hear your thoughts, dreams and visions—not to mention your feelings on what I have written so far. I wish they would let us correspond freely, without such long silences between our expressions of love. I want the two of us to get on with our separate, but combined lives. I need some soft and warm words from one loved once and still. Nothing here can supply me with anything that only you offer. I have spent many nights conceiving of ways to escape this caged hell. I'm even getting used to the bars, though their reality screams loud and clear in the drained, empty caverns of my subconscious. Please write, write until your fingers bleed or beyond, until the muscles of your body deny your brain the passage for it to convey to me its messages!

"P.S. In addition to your emotional responses, please send me some food."

It appears that my tentmates have been silenced by their own annoyance. They sit quietly and appear to be in thought. I am isolated from them for I wish to be as alone as one can be—without actually being alone.

I am far from everything—from civilization, friends, loved ones, and all that matters to me. I sit in a tent in a desert that held nothing until we arrived. Then it held nothing but us—and sand. I am alone among thousands of others; we're alone together. It doesn't matter how many people there are in a desert; when you're in one, you're alone. I'm separated from all the other loners. I maintain my sanity alone, though leaving here will take the help of thousands—thousands of people who are just as alone as I am.

Loneliness is a place where fish don't swim, flowers have no smell and birds lose
    their wings.
It is a land with many inhabitants, though no two are friends.
Loneliness is where the sun once set and has yet to return.
The people there have plenty of food though never possess the hunger.
These people have plenty to say though there is no one who will ever listen.

Loneliness has streams and rivers though they have no place to flow.
The people are able to laugh though nothing is ever funny.
Loneliness is not a foreign country, state, nor province,
Loneliness is on no map that I know.
But loneliness is a place we easily find, when it is our time to go.

We got a dart board today. It started out as a healthy pastime, until we learned the fun of throwing darts at things other than the board—such as military equipment, MREs, the tent, rats, water bottles and each other.

I didn't want this war to start, but since it has, I wish we'd hurry up and win so we can all get on with our lives. Some will surely die, and those who do escape with their lives must live for themselves and for all of those who didn't make it.

This vast nothingness is playing with my mind. Even driving from A to B can leave you feeling hopeless. Being in a truck on the sand is like being in a boat on the ocean. There are no points of reference. The only helpful landmarks are tire tracks—millions of lines in the sand that tell you other people are around. If you don't see tracks, you better find some quickly. I often feel like a piece of paper floating aimlessly with no hope of reaching shore. If it weren't for a few tracks in the sand there would be 500,000 lost soldiers roaming around this desert, never to be found. When it rains, which is more often that one would expect, the tire tracks disappear. We have to start from scratch. It's hard to convey terror in words. The next time you're swimming in the ocean, close your eyes, spin yourself around to get disoriented. Then try to find a paper cup somewhere on the beach. That is close—though it doesn't convey the fear we have of meeting the enemy or driving over a land mine.

When I was in civilization, I was able to look ahead, plan for the future. Here I find it difficult to predict the next minute, let alone tomorrow or next year.

February 6, 1991. Today I felt as if I was in a M*A*S*H episode. I visited a full-blown military hospital. The sights and sounds seemed right out of the TV show.

February 7, 1991. I awoke this morning with a burning hatred for anyone who feels he has to ask me what's wrong. An officer approached me and asked what was bothering me, because I looked a bit out of sorts. I looked right at him and asked if he had any more questions. I surely have more answers. He turned and walked away quite aware of my plight.

February 8, 1991. Nothing!

February 9, 1991. Once again I was able to use the phones. Someone has been very nice about letting us use them so often. Maybe they're doing it to prevent us from killing each other. I was able to reach one of my best friends in the States. It was around four in the morning back home, but I didn't wake him. The phone rang, and he answered breathlessly. The operator told him who it was and where I was calling from. Then I heard him tell somebody to get off of him. We laughed about it. Near the end of the conversation, he even turned the phone over to his company. I stood in the desert talking to a girl who was a total stranger and probably totally naked as well. It was an odd feeling. God! I hate this place!

I also talked to a friend in New York. She said she had sent me something to wear around my neck, a patron saint of good travels. I am not religious at all, but I can use all the help I can get.

When talking to people on the phone I often remind them to speak to me as their friend, not as someone in a war. I can't stand to be patronized. Now that I am here, I believe I can handle the truth.

As I wrote that last entry I watched a flat round piece of metal travel from my horizon, past me and off into the distance. It traveled over hills and under trucks, never stopping for more than the time needed to figure out how to pass an obstacle. It traveled in a happy way, it seemed to bounce and flop around as if it was enjoying itself. I can't imagine how many miles it has crossed and will cross before something stops it. The poetry and symbolism it possesses is beautiful and appropriate. At times I feel like that lost piece,

Be prepared—As the shooting drew nearer, the GIs repeatedly packed and repacked their gear

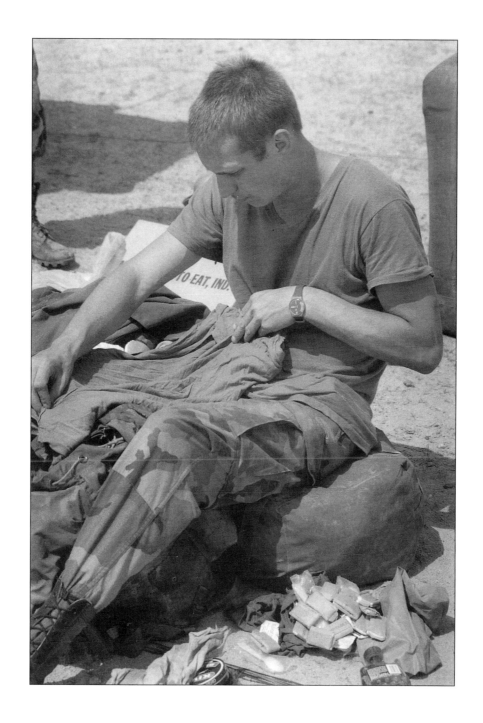

floating across this desert—and this life—not knowing where I am going. All I have are blurred memories of the thousands of places I've been.

The difference between poetry and prose is this: Poetry resembles a literary sculpture in which the process of seeing is built into its structure. The artist controls the entire work, and it is slowly revealed to its viewer. Prose is a literary painting. The viewer can grasp the entire concept at once, enabling him to ponder its entirety. Then he is able to construct his own interpretation of it.

February 10, 1991. Good morning. It is my turn to sit inside by the stove while the others are out on Stand Two. I have the pleasure of burning shit today, which means I'm exempt from the morning cold. The only way to get out of participating in one evil chore around here is to be picked for one much worse.

Every morning, as everyone crawls back into the tent and prepares breakfast, an interesting ritual takes place. I am not sure when it began or why. But while we eat our wonderful breakfasts, we abuse each other verbally. We put each other down for an hour or two and ridicule anyone and everyone in our tent. I guess it lets us release our hatreds so we are able to perform together in a half decent fashion.

Earlier I had to venture across the patch of desert that lies between our camp and the one next door. It was an enjoyable stroll. I brought my Walkman along. We're not allowed to do this, but I tucked it away nicely. The musical selection for the trip was by Bach. As I walked through nothing I reveled in the beauty of this music. I felt as if I was the music, I saw nothing. It was truly a new way to experience this beauty—though I'd exchange it for visual distraction at the drop of a dime. But I'm here, so I have to find beauty wherever I can.

I've been corresponding with a friend in Germany. The funny thing about this correspondence is that the order of things has been anything but correct. She numbers each letter she writes. A letter takes three to six weeks to travel one way. The first one I received was #3, the next was #5 then followed #2 and #4. I've just been delivered #1. Either someone is playing a joke or someone doesn't have a chance in hell of ever being called good at their job!

February 11, 1991. The division psychiatrist arrived today to observe how we're dealing with battle fatigue. She'll be spending the night. Well, we have yet to see a battle. And the fatigue we suffer is from activities that are meant to keep us busy so we won't shoot each other. We're closer to being at war with each other than with Iraq.

A soldier in my tent summed things up well when he said, "In the Army, it's not that you are you, and they are them. You're better off if they are them and you want to be like them."

The officers have what is called staff call every evening, when they are supposed to discuss and plan for the war. Well, they've had some spare time and used it to create a stooge-of-the-week award called the Bedouin Boner. It's a camel bone attached to a rope that the winner must wear to each meeting for a week. This week's winner: a Captain who mistook his urinal for orange Kool-Aid. Will anyone follow this man into battle?

Instead of drowning in the deep waters of our futures, we float on the surface of the present and enjoy each other's humor—the ultimate defense against the storm. Yes a storm, and we'll bear the brunt of it in a matter of days. I don't even have my yellow windbreaker. Like I said, we're using humor to shield ourselves from the truth!

My writing seem to be dragging along, but then so does everything else.

February 12, 1991. We received word that we are to move forward—and were told to prepare for the worst. If all goes as planned, we'll be in Iraq nine days from now. We've taken the camouflage from the tents and vehicles so we don't have to bother with them when we pull out. The funny thing about the camo nets is that they're dark green and meant for heavily wooded areas. They insisted we put them up to hide the dark green tents. Incredible!

In the process of taking down the nets, I was hoisted up on top of our tent. I felt like a fiddler on the roof.

With the care that is put into someone's last meal we pack once more, for it may be our last chance to pack correctly. Every step toward this war is a step toward home—if we don't get shot waiting in line.

Our atmosphere is happy-like. I attribute that to finally doing something. We've been stagnant far too long. It's time to cry and go home or face the bully. Either way, starting something is the only way to end this, which is all we care about. When I use the term "us" I am not implying a general association. When I say "we" I mean me and the guy next to me, and the guys I've grown close to these past days.

I'm waiting for the day when I'll no longer count up to war, but down to home.

As the evening shortens, so do our tempers. The air is thick with latrine-derived theories. One could slice a wedge from the air in this tent and pass it off as yesterday's chow. It's that tough.

While I was packing I came across something I forgot I had with me. It's a small box of letters and photographs that go wherever I go. I believe that Robert Fulgrum refers to this as a "Gummy Lump." It's a small collection of shameless love accumulated over the years. I was aware that I had brought the lump, but I was unaware of its contents.

Among the riches I found a greeting card I received from a young lady of sixteen when I was a whopping seventeen. It has an Oriental design that anyone would be proud of, though the inside is decorated in a way that only she could.

The card isn't filled with proper Hallmark sentiments. No. It contains the only expressions that fit—hers. She was a year younger than I, but in other ways she was a grown woman in a world that I hadn't even seen yet.

At first, rumor had us moving out to another assembly area tomorrow. It now appears that we will move in a few days. They keep telling us things that scare us, then they dangle them in front of our faces like cheese, making sure we're total wrecks. Isn't it enough that we fear our enemy? Why must we fear our own side as well? I'm not exaggerating when I say that most of us have more than minor reservations about some of our leaders.

This evening I got a letter from my brother, the first he has ever written to me. Reading it was devastating; his words of love and concern have thrown me for a loop. I wasn't expecting this from him—and surely not a day or two before we move forward. I am lonely, missing life and unsure of my future.

Mailed December 12, 1990, received January 12, 1991:

> Dear Geoff,
> I just got done watching the Congressional debate over whether to authorize the President's use of force against Iraq, if he deems it necessary. As they passed the resolution, it hit me that I was watching something happening that was far away, but that couldn't have an impact closer to home. I guess that is what finally caused me to get off of my duff and write to

you. I realized that this may be the last chance I get to talk to you. I apologize that it takes something as serious as this to get me to write you, but as you know, I don't write letters often. Please do not think for one minute that I have forgotten about you or that I am not concerned about the situation in which you have landed. My thoughts are with you as you enter into this conflict. I am not sure how to feel about 'why' you are there. I want you to know that I believe in what is trying to be accomplished, even though I wish you were not directly involved.

I hope that you are home safe as soon as possible. I am really looking forward to a time when you and I are living and working in the same city, so our relationship can continue to flourish. You are the best brother a guy could ask for, and I love you. Besides, half the time you are the only one who gets my jokes.

So here I am, sitting in the desert, packing for war. I stand still, for his words come from another reality, the one that I left behind, the one that enables me to withstand the present one. My brother often shudders at revealing his emotions, but my situation has forced him to. Part of him is here with me. I've always felt strongly about him, though it is forbidden to express such feelings when they make the other side uncomfortable. His emotions have stirred my own, and the feeling is refreshing, though it angers me as well. If I die we will never be able to savor those feelings as our friendship and brotherhood evolve through life. If I die, it will be over before we had time to grow together.

Mike, if I die before I can answer your letter, I'm sorry. You deserved better, I love you.

My brother once said to me, "It is one thing to accomplish the writing of a book, quite another to accomplish something with what you have written.

"Not the least of my problems is that I can hardly imagine what kind of an experience a genuine, self-authenticating religious experience would be. Without somehow destroying myself in the process, how could God reveal himself in a way that would leave no room for doubt? If there is no room for doubt, there would be no room for me."

I've answered my brother's letter. It was too important to leave until later. I wrote that our parents had raised us well—very well—though I can't look deep enough into my past to find any moral lesson that could help me in this situation. I can't imagine what I could have been taught that would have prepared me for it. The next few days will show how good or bad our training has been. But this—surviving at the edge of the abyss—was never taught. I don't think I could learn it. And if I did, could I return to my other life once it's over?

February 13, 1991. We're leaving tomorrow and glad of it. We're so tired of being trapped in one place. We're packing again, and playing around with the chores we have to endure, trying to have fun wherever possible. One would never think we could be in good spirits at this delicately balanced point, but we are. Anything is better than an indefinite prison sentence in this camp.

The big trucks that carved the trenches in our new home have returned to patch up the wounds, though the land will forever bare the scars. They never did get around to completing the swimming pool.

It's interesting to watch the process of preparing for war. Few of us have ever done it before but everyone is running around doing exactly what is needed and expected. Maybe we're just scattering about trying to figure out what to do. Either way there's a lot of movement.

We're scheduled to pull out at 0800, a few hours from now. We'll spend half the time resting and the other half running madly around. One more time, we're checking and re-checking what we've already packed and repacked.

We're sitting around with nothing to do. It's late. We're ready to leave except for the last-minute things that can't be done until we pull out. We're spending our last moments of peace and pseudo relaxation discussing who will play us in the film of this war. We disagree on most of the characters, though everyone thinks I should be portrayed by Matthew Broderick. Maybe. I just hope that he isn't playing me in the past tense.

Change number 2001: We're getting up at 0200 to do the remaining chores and pull out by 0600. Why are the good things always postponed, and the bad ones moved up?

Hurry up and wait—The ground assault was occasionally stalled by local residents

I'll be driving a deuce-and-a-half truck into Iraq. My codriver is a very religious female sergeant. At the end of this, we will either be the best of friends or the worst of enemies. Only time will tell, and we'll certainly have plenty.

I'm lying here with Bach in my ears, glancing around the tent and realizing that it has become a home. I don't mean that in the usual way the term is used. I mean something much more important. I came here a grown man, but I leave a bigger one. And I'm going to a place where I can expect to grow even more. I've learned things about myself and others that no other place could have taught me. For this reason I shall forever despise and love this place. To see this tent dismantled is to say goodbye to memories and love— yes love. Don't ask me how, why or who; I just feel a love for something here.

With departure almost on us, I will end with this quote:

"The most shocking fact about war is that its victims and its instruments are human beings, and that these individual beings are condemned by the monstrous conventions of politics to murder or be murdered in quarrels not their own."[13]

PART SIX

Everyone Knows But Us

February 14, 1991. Sitting, waiting, I see hundreds of trucks coming from everywhere to join us. We are big! The sight of this is something the world will never forget. I would hate to be on the receiving end of it.

Oh great! I was just informed that the last time my Division was in a desert on Valentines day, they got their butts kicked. Terrific! I feel much better now.

We're moving. Every time there's a slight change in the land's contour, I see trucks stretching to the horizon in every direction. That's encouraging. Since I can't see the beginning or the end of this vast convoy, I must be in the middle. That's good—unless the enemy aims for the middle.

We're making a gigantic pit stop. Everyone is dashing out of their trucks, to relieve themselves and release pent-up energy. They scurry to other trucks to discuss what we've just experienced. They share information to justify what they believe they just saw.

After driving across the flattest land I've ever seen, we've stopped in front of a big canyon. It's a wadi, a big hole carved into the earth by water. There's an oasis at the bottom, but the sides of the wadi are steep and sandy, too loose for our trucks. The place looks like a death trap.

After sitting for an hour and a half, someone with a lot of brass on his uniform drove

Tailgate party—GIs watch from trucktops as the division launches an artillery barrage. For many, this was all they saw of the fighting in Desert Storm

down and through the wadi, which turned out to be less dangerous than it seemed. As we passed through, I noticed a small village among the trees. It looked like a ghost town. Trucks, houses, and children's toys were abandoned, as though everyone stopped what they were doing and split. There were cars with their motors still running, and water faucets left flowing. In the middle of the street were dolls and bicycles. Everyone simply vanished. Whoever lived there left in a big hurry. I even noticed a dog whose leash was tied to a tree. I wonder what happened. It gave me the chills!

It's evening, and we've stopped to rest for a day. Our next move is to a staging area near the border.

We've been told that our plan of attack is a sneaky one. The Iraqis are expecting us to enter their country through Kuwait from Saudi Arabia. That is exactly what we want them to think, but it's not the plan. We're going out of our way, to the left of Kuwait, entering Iraq on the bottom left and scooping up their Republican Guard in Northern Kuwait. This will trap them, keeping them from running north to Baghdad. That, at least, is what we've been told.

Today we received a popular international newspaper. It had a full-color map and graph showing the exact plans I just wrote about. The diagram had every last detail, including which units are involved, how many soldiers in each unit, and the types of weapons the units have. What the hell is this? Why would they be allowed to print that? What if Saddam reads this paper. All he has to do is meet us at the border. It would be one thing if the printing of that map was meant to confuse Saddam. But those are our exact intentions. Couldn't they have printed another plan? I need someone to explain this to me.

Earlier today as we traveled across the desert, three Scuds were fired at the King Khalid Military City. That is a place where soldiers from all units and all countries involved in this conflict go for food, rest and supplies. We were just told that the explosions we heard were made by Patriot missiles blowing the Scuds out of the sky. The Patriot missile was not made to destroy other missiles in flight, but I don't care. If I own a dog in the future I'll call him Patriot.

I'm watching a man sew many plastic MRE coverings together. He's making a waterproof mat for sleeping on the ground. It's amazing what you can come up with when you have to. Another soldier is aimlessly wondering all over the camp. I noticed him earlier but thought nothing of him. It's an hour later, and he hasn't stopped. He walks with his head down and appears to be mumbling to himself. I think I'll join him. I'm due for an aimless stroll.

Certain songs and types of music have always conjured up specific memories for me, memories that lift me up and put a smile on my face. But now these songs have been wrenched from their moorings in my mind. After hearing them out here, on this beach from Hell, they will always remind me of Desert Storm.

One of our adopted fathers—Wade, who is a cross between Willy Nelson and Dennis Hopper—is a true child of the 1960s. His laid-back way of handling this desert life is admired by many. He walks around and comforts others when they need it. He speaks his mind in a way that eases people's spirits.

Tonight I must sleep in this ambulance, wedged in with three other people. We just shook hands and asked each other to be our Valentines.

February 15, 1991. Often I have mentioned that certain places and events did not hold the type of feeling or atmosphere one would expect from a war. We have guns and tanks, there are thousands of soldiers running around, and the radio continues to cry war. But we don't look and act like a military operation. We're more like a bunch of professional street punks, hired to beat up on someone's little sister or conduct a massive robbery of lunch money—not a war!

But if the war doesn't feel quite real, the fear does. I fear that acting like the war will be a cakewalk endangers our lives. If it turns out to be easier than we thought, fine! But there is nothing easy about being here. We could be in for a rude awakening. On one hand we are told the fighting will be easy; on the other we're told that 50,000 soldiers are expected to die in the first month of battle. That does not sound like a cakewalk.

This morning, I went in search of the dreaded latrine. Everyone guided me to a long line over a hill. I joined it with trepidation. Then it was my turn, and a soldier pointed out my destination—four poles wrapped with fabric, no more than three feet high. Inside was a metal folding chair with a circular hole in the seat, perched over a deep, very full hole. I was able to ignore the stench, because the low walls let me look around and observe everyone's reactions—and, of course, they observed mine.

I was told that today is Friday. Most of us are lying around entertaining ourselves with cards, trying to get clean, reading army manuals and listening to songs we can recite from memory.

Earlier today the radio said that Saddam had supposedly agreed to comply with UN sanctions. But Saddam is not the most trusted man in these parts. America responded by saying that his words came too late. The only way we'll stop the attack is if Iraq physically pulls out of Kuwait.

Saddam went on the radio to address his people. He told them that it was all over. After that, British news reported that the people of Baghdad were celebrating in the streets. We stared at each other in confusion. We were looking for answers, but no one gave us any. For a few moments it seemed that our mission was accomplished, that we wouldn't have to fight. We reached for that dream, knowing deep down it wasn't true.

February 16, 1991. Ah, another morning in the desert! Sometimes every day seems like a clone of a dozen previous days. But today's dawn brings us closer to Iraq. Today is different.

I'm sitting in the cab of my truck awaiting any kind of movement. We planned to leave hours ago. Maybe someone forgot the directions. It's a long way across tough terrain. There's no point in pondering what today will hold for us. There's no way of knowing and no way to avoid it.

I'll have to quit smoking in a day or two—not for my health, but because I'm running out of cigarettes and we haven't passed a whole hell of a lot of 7-Elevens lately.

This procession reminds me of a wagon train in the Old West. But instead of looking for a new homes on the empty prairies, we're invading someone else's homeland to kill them. Come to think of it, maybe we are like the settlers, invading Indian territory with the intention of eradicating them.

We're finally moving again, but so slowly it barely registers on the speedometer. I fell asleep while my partner drove. I must have had an incredible dream, because I woke up angry.

Boy, what a trip! We drove all day through a flat, endless landscape so boring that even the drivers fell asleep. But the last 30 minutes have snapped us to attention—and of course, I was behind the wheel. After the flats, we encountered an area of small hills. My truck was too big to avoid the hills so I steered through, around, and at times, over them.

It wasn't too difficult until one hill tried to devour the truck in a sand slide. We almost tipped over. Everyone survived, and we are spending the break rushing around discussing the mishap.

Finally, we're in the staging area—the last stop before Iraq. A small step for the military, but a giant last leap for some of us. I wonder how long we'll have to wait here. We've traveled too far for too long, and have had to deal with too many emotions to turn back now—even if we could.

February 17, 1991. Desert Storm is one month old today, and I haven't had a chance to shop for a gift!

We were told that we'll remain here five days, then move into Iraq. The alternative is to stay here until we're sent home. That would mean a very long wait.

Once again we're constructing a camp, but this time we're not building for comfort. Everything is for speed and efficiency. We should be able to pack up and move in no time flat. That means living out of our duffel bags. I feel like a bag lady.

This place is different for another reason. Every moment we spend here is torture. Some are calling it Death Row.

I just returned from washing my canteen cup free of corrosives like MREs and Army coffee. While I was consumed by the task I heard an unusual sound and saw about a dozen people and the chaplain huddled around a truck holding their rifles. They were singing religious songs. The sound was strange and uncomfortably haunting. It seems so strange to me—people believing they're here for God's purpose, that God wants them here. To me this is a case of the nonexistent leading the blind.

I washed off a few layers of desert crud, though I still look and feel filthy. I miss the smells of cleanliness: perfumed soaps, colognes—not to mention household aromas like a fireplace or the scent of dinner cooking. I long for the comforting feeling of turning off that last light in the house before I snuggle into bed, falling asleep in the arms of someone who cares. Right now I would even settle for someone who doesn't care. I miss the sound

Saddle up!—After months of waiting, 500,000 U.S. ground troops begin their lightning sweep through Iraq and Kuwait

of a toilet flushing as the water swishes around the bowl. Most of all I feel the absence of freedom to do, think, and go where I wish. I want to be able to say, "No!" without going to jail.

February 18, 1991. A few of us are sitting around the tent listening to music, letting the words and melodies take us far from this place. The rest are washing up. The chaplain is here getting his hair cut by one of the few people who own clippers. He bribed the barber with a lollipop.

Today was hectic. We're sitting around for the first time all day, except for a brief lunch. Each of us has an opinion about what lies ahead. The predictions have changed drastically since we left Germany. Now we're frightened by all the possibilities. We all feel that there is no way to avoid the horror any more. We're perched on the edge of Hell waiting for a signal. I'm scared. Breathing becomes harder each day.

I've been here for so long that at times I find myself identifying a person from a hundred meters away simply by his walk. I can also interpret that person's emotional state. Soldiers who are OK walk on top of the sand with ease. Those who are depressed seem to walk below the surface, kicking up a cloud with each step.

A friend just told me he was going to the pisser. He left me and began walking in that direction. After a few steps his head lowered and he lost his bearings. Then he walked past the pisser about four hundred meters from the camp. When he looked up and finally saw where he was, he set a new course. Once again, he was off course a few minutes later; then he walked up to me and asked how I was doing. I said, "I'm fine. And how are you?" He replied that he felt a bit down and that he had to urinate. Then he said he would try to find the pisser later when his mind was more clear. As he walked away he said, "I hope I can stop thinking long enough to find my tent."

Earlier today we packed our aid bags with assortments of life-saving equipment. What we're allowed to carry is useless for anything more than a stubbed toe. We had asked if we were going to carry morphine in case we came across a serious injury. The answer was No. What are we supposed to do for a guy whose arm is ten feet away? Sing him a lullaby?

February 19, 1991. A jet fighter buzzed the camp early this morning. We were frightened out of our skins. It was a friendly plane, but who can tell in the dark? At first it sounded like an incoming Scud. We were all under our cots by the time we recognized it as a plane.

Don't ask me how, but the mailman was here. There was nothing for me personally, though we all got enough army mail to last a lifetime. I'm sitting here in a pile of Valentine cards. We've all received countless season's greeting from strangers and now, countless unknown children are asking us to be their Valentines.

It seems that every elementary school in the United States has required their students to write us, and we are all sick and tired of hearing how people at home understand. I'm sitting with ten or more letters in my lap, all beginning with some version of, "Don't ask what your country can do for you, blah, blah, blah!" If I read that one more time I'll be ill. My friend who went home on emergency leave rejoined us today. He brought us candy bars and stories from the States.

We've been informed that we will not leave any sooner that the 24th of this month. Possibly later. I heard via the grapevine that there are talks being held somewhere to avoid this ground attack. If they're successful, we'll be sitting here longer than I care to sit. I don't mind if there is a way to avoid entering Iraq, though I do mind sitting here indefinitely, like an idiot being stood up for a date and not having the common sense to go home.

February 20, 1991. Today is my second anniversary in this man's Army. No presents, please. I was handed a can of gasoline and told to go burn shit.

Last night we experienced a violent storm. We were awakened about three in the morning by thunder, lightning and enough rain to launch Noah's Ark. We jumped out of bed and into action, each person doing something to insure that our home remained standing. One secured the tent poles, another pulled cots away from the sides. I ran out to confront the storm with a shovel and dig up enough dirt to bury the side of the tent. In the process, I dug a moat large enough to require a crossing bridge. Then we tried to sleep, expecting at any moment that the tent would become a kite.

In the morning, personal belongings were scattered everywhere. The day has been full of storytelling. Some people woke up with three feet of water in their tents. One guy told me that he woke up when his cot floated into another.

No matter how well you know someone, when you live with them under such close conditions, there are sure to be surprises. Those who are calm can become aggressive;

those who are assholes are known to be nice on occasion—but not as often as nice people change into assholes.

February 21, 1991. I'm sitting in a Ford Bronco, listening to Walt Disney's *Fantasia* and watching shit burn. I swindled another carton of smokes so my habit reigns. Smoking is the only thing that keeps me going. I have no idea how people who don't smoke can manage here. A lot of people who came as nonsmokers have picked up the habit.

Lately, I've felt that there was nothing worth writing about anymore. My physical surroundings are boring, my life uneventful. It's as if this were the only life I've ever known. What was new, awkward and exciting has become monotonous. Nothing seems unusual when I sit down to document this experience.

I must be blessed. I got two packages today. Their contents were trivial, except for one item—a cassette tape of Man of La Mancha. I've been waiting a long time for this. The thought of going into battle without it was frightening. Now I have all my toys. I'm giddy, ready for war.

I also got another tape—the musical 1776. I listened to it until I reached a depressing song called "Mama Look Sharp." I'll never listen to it again. It's about a soldier in a battlefield, keeping his head down and calling for his mother.

We're balanced on a rope that is fraying one strand at a time. We can see it happening, feel each strand as it's torn by the daily tension. One day, the strands will be gone. Then we'll be hurled into Hell. For now, our lives are a balancing act.

Sometimes I can't react emotionally, I simply ignore things. When I have to deal with an overpowering emotion, I shut off. A kind of autopilot takes over. I wonder if it has a backup. I may need it.

We have a little friend in our tent, a field mouse that found his way in and can't get out. Every few minutes he stops and looks around as if waiting for me to show him the exit. He looks frustrated and confused. Hey little buddy, if I knew the way out of here I would have used it.

February 23, 1991. Well the Militant God has spoken. The ground attack begins tomorrow. For the hundredth and last time we adjust, rearrange, pack and repack all we can—and then some. We were issued commercial packaged meals, like Dinty Moore and

Hormel, which were distributed in the normal military way—every man for himself. People attacked the pile like savages until there was nothing left but cardboard boxes.

Soldiers have begun altering their vehicles and load plans for comfort and convenience. Rules and regulations no longer apply. If we're going to war, we must be comfortable. The compartments under my seat on the side of my truck, were once filled with manuals and useless tools. Now they are packed with food, clothes, and journals. These things are important to my survival. They're my essentials.

Last night I cleaned my rifle for the first time since I got to the desert—cleaned it like no other has ever been cleaned before. It's ready for battle, but I'm not sure I'm capable of using it to take another's life, even in self-defence. I don't know if I'll ever be able to do that, and I don't wish to find out. How could I kill someone else's father, brother, son? This evening is our last one in safety, and we're spending it in silence. On previous such occasions, we were able to find a lightness within ourselves. Tonight the weight is far too heavy.

There's one element that allowed other fearful nights to be less ominous. We knew that they weren't The night, that there was still time before the shooting started. Tonight the fear is palpable. No one is crying Wolf any more. The wolf is here. When the sun comes up, we'll go after him him. I not only hear the beast breathing, I can smell him.

PART SEVEN

Dominion of the Wolf

February 24, 1991. With our lives packed on our wheels, we wait to invade the predator's territory—tense and frozen, like foxes at the instant they know they're being hunted.

I'm seated in my truck, my wartime home, looking at an endless line of vehicles pointed at Iraq. I'm abstracted, excited, but weak and vulnerable in face of what might befall us. What will become of me and my friends? Will we live or die? Will we kill? Will we cry?

As I sit in front of the AR's open door I can hear the shenanigans of its occupants. I don't want to enter. I want to go home. This is one experience I can do without. The others are trying to relax, but you can sense the tension beneath the surface. Some appear hyped-up, eager to take on the wolf. Is this possible? Or are they just so scared that they disguise the fear with bravado?

We are spending these last few moments trying to perfect our readiness—like runners digging in at the starting blocks. Our footholds are as secure as possible, but that is no guarantee. On this track there are no guarantees.

We're leaving in minutes, but we still had to perform two of the dumbest chores this Army has yet conjured up. The first had us filling us our foxholes. There are hundreds of huge holes all over this desert. Why they want us to fill in some of them—not all, just a random few—is beyond comprehension. The second aimless exercise is called Police

Grisly rout—Much of the Iraqi army dissolved in panic before the American assault, simply abandoning their dead and wounded. The driver of one retreating tank didn't even bother to steer around a fallen comrade

Call. The entire unit forms a long, straight line and walks forward picking up trash. What bothers me is that the desert is filled with trash—not entirely of our making. It's apparently impolite to litter the country you're defending. What about all the bombs, the land mines, the corpses? They're OK, but trash is a No-No.

With moments between us and the unknown, we were summoned to the pep rally to end all pep rallies. Our commander tried his best to deliver a proper go-out-and-kick-ass speech, but he fell just short of rendering us Last Rites. I walked away confused about how to feel after such a display.

I'm in my truck. Since Saddam might use chemical weapons, we're all wearing our protective suits. The interesting and aggravating thing is that we were ordered to use the ones we ruined when we first got to the desert, no good for anything but a garage sale. I need someone to explain this one to me—NOW!

Well, I just got the explanation. I was told "just because the suit got wet and the protective layer has been washed away doesn't mean that the suit is no good." I asked why they call that missing layer the "protective" layer. The answer: they think that if we are attacked with chemicals, the suit would provide enough protection to enable us to seek shelter and change into another suit. What? You think! Where's the science in all of this?

There has been some movement here and there as we merge into a huge, wedge-shaped mass of hundreds of thousands of soldiers and vehicles. Our unit is at the center, protected on all sides. But there is always the possibility of incoming artillery. So it is comforting to be surrounded by such a force, even though we're a desirable target. We control all of the other units. You might say we have the flag.

Later. We have traveled a ways. I'm not sure where we are in relation to Iraq, but we must be close. I just rushed back to the truck. I was sitting between two trucks with a cloth dangling across them, on a chair with a hole in it, relieving myself with one hand on my protective mask and my pants around my ankles—one foot on the toilet paper and the other maintaining balance, one hand holding the cloth so it wouldn't get blown away.

Once more, with feeling—Another barrage, another chance to feel more like a witness to, than a veteran of, Desert Storm

Then the cloth was yanked away, people started shouting at me to hurry, and the two trucks started to pull apart. I was left on display as I scrambled to get dressed and run back to my truck. What an experience.

We've stopped again. From where I'm sitting I can see Iraq through a big barrier of sand and rock that has already been broken for our passage. The next sentence I write will be from Iraq.

February 24, 1991. It's dark now. We stopped for the evening after quite a day. We have ventured almost forty miles across difficult terrain. Immediately after we entered Iraq my emotions and fears changed as drastically as the landscape altered. Saudi Arabia was flat and smooth, but here it's rocky and unpredictable.

I'd give anything not to be here. I keep hoping we'll be granted a reprieve. I take back anything I ever said or did to offend anyone. How can I sleep on the edge of doom? How can I think happy thoughts when the next thought could be my last? I've learned many things in the Army—weapons, survival, even saving lives—but nothing I've ever experienced has taught me how to deal with this moment.

Earlier I wrote about driving in tactical blackout—that's when you travel at night with no light except two microscopic blinkers in the front and two red ones in the rear. Now we won't even have those. My truck got stuck briefly in the dark, and by the time I freed it, I couldn't see the truck in front of me, though I was aware of those behind me. I threw on a pair of night-vision goggles—and made it clear to my passenger that finding our unit was more important to me than the vanity of driving smoothly. I then slammed the truck forward without regard to possible obstacles. A few minutes and dents later we were back with the unit, but it was an anxious time.

Our destination is an area north of Kuwait inside Iraq, where a group of Saddam's elite forces are reported. Our mission is to "dispose" of them. I love that word. We were warned of resistance along the way. I wonder how long it will be before we're shooting at people. I can feel the carnivores breathing on my neck.

Firepower—This was once the turret of an Iraqi tank. It was blown some 50 feet from the rest of the vehicle

February 25, 1991. It's 6:00 A.M. The sun is struggling to face the day, hiding behind the security of clouds.

My travel partner and I have been marking the miles and events on the back of our seats with a permanent marker. The interior of the vehicle is beginning to resemble a bathroom stall. We've been in this country a whole day, and no one has even thrown a rock at us. What's going on? Is it possible that they really don't know we're here? Any minute I expect to see thousands of Iraqi troops pop out from the sand shouting, "Surprise!"

Recalling yesterday, I think about the first minutes after we entered Iraq. All the vehicles had stopped for a short break. We welcomed each other to Iraq and to the war. I, among others, found great pleasure in taking a moment to urinate on this country. The satisfaction lasted no longer than the act.

Many soldiers seem to be running about in nervous excitement, not knowing what to feel or expect. We're in a war, in a land that promises pain and death, destruction and murder, and so far we've seen nothing but ourselves. I wonder where the war is. Every step I take I think will be my last, but my confusion keeps me from the fright that makes people shit in their shorts.

Fifty miles have passed, and my emotions have settled somewhat. The scene is as follows: I'm sitting on the roof of my truck looking around at every swinging dick perched on his vehicle. We've climbed up for a better view, because the rocket launchers are about to fire. One would think that the safest thing to do would be to seek shelter in case they return our fire. Not us. Drivers are sitting on their vehicles as far as the eye can see in every direction.

It looks like a college tailgate party. It's a football game, and we're the visiting team. Saddam and the Iraqis have been penalized for delay of game, face-masking, being off-sides, and unsportsmanlike conduct. We've have been penalized for unnecessary roughness, out-of-bounds, clipping and having too many players on the field. Iraq has the ball in terrible field position. We're trying for a safety.

Funny thing. Our Seventh Corps symbol, which we display on all our vehicles, looks like a team logo. We even wear it on our clothing, like a varsity letter.

As each rocket is launched, a brilliant flash of light is followed by a deafening crash. I see silhouettes of my comrades sitting on their trucks. I can even see a herd of camels in the flashes. We're on a safari with fireworks. This is a theme park, a drive-through experience for the whole family.

I have taken photographs in many of the countries I have visited, but this is my only war, so the photos are priceless. I want to share the images, so those who have been here and even those who will never see this, can get an fraction of the experience. I imagine the newspapers are showing a lot of destruction. I doubt that the images are ever from the soldier's viewpoint.

February 26, 1991. The explosions and flashes of light continued even as we rested. Thousands of Iraqi soldiers were being murdered. I'm not basing this on news reports. I know the destructive capabilities of the weapons our unit has been firing—and their accuracy. I doesn't take a genius to figure out what's happening on the receiving end.

During our long wait for this moment, we were constantly informed of our enemy's capabilities. The statisticians predicted that fifty to 100 American soldiers would be killed in the first week or two of the ground war. From listening to the tactical radio, I have heard that there has been little to no resistance. Why? Has the air attack demolished everything? I doubt that. I've heard that Saddam has been treating his soldiers like peasants—no food, inappropriate clothing, scarce medical support—and lies. Maybe the Iraqi soldiers have nothing to fight for—but still, I would think they'd rather fight than sit still and welcome death.

The radio has been encouraging—victorious battles we can't see, and news that Iraqi soldiers are surrendering left and right. I would like to believe it, but I'm suspicious of propaganda. I can't feel joy, even though it looks good for our side. I'd just rather be alive than dead when all of this is over.

This morning we had our first encounter with real, not imagined danger. Our travels brought us to a mine field. We were instructed to drive in the tire tracks of the vehicles in front. That's great, but what about the people in front? I hope everyone's underwear is clean.

Ghost town—The Iraqi city of Messila was reduced to rubble by the bombardment.

113

114

We move in a predictable pattern—move a little, stop a lot and fire even more. When we hear of threats ahead, we stop. Some rest, others relieve themselves. A few find the courage to eat MRE's. No matter what rituals we perform, we all watch our missiles illuminate the sky.

The light show somehow brings on memories of good times. We listen to the radio's news of mass destruction, surrenders, press conferences with good reports. Is it possible that this is a war? I hear that American casualties are light. In the big picture, our side has lost a few, but the outlook is good. Still I remain pessimistic. I don't believe it. The war is passing me by, but there will probably be a second pass. Will we be so lucky the next time around?

There has been some heavy fighting at the outer edges of our wedge. It's night, and I can see flashes of confrontation on both sides and in front. I hear the radio scream out cries for support, and see movement within the ranks to give it. Until this moment, I was content in my semisafety. But as I hear the cries of others, I wish there was something I could do. I don't want to kill. I'd rather help the fallen. I'm a medic. The radio said that the war could be over by the end of the month, which is just a few days away. I'll believe that when it happens.

One of the eerie things about this experience is that the sky has been cloudy ever since we entered Iraq. As I look around I can see people praying, sleeping, reading, listening to music or news, or thinking. I'm just sitting here being scared and waiting for word to move out.

I'm not sure of the time, but it's hours later. We had to make a hasty move north to stop and dig in during a sandstorm that shows no signs of relenting. We expect an attack. My passenger and I have finished our hole. I'm looking around, watching people dig like they've never dug before. Sand is flying up from the ground and into the sandstorm.

It was a false alarm. Shortly after the holes were dug, we packed up and moved. Now we're somewhere near Kuwait. After we arrived, I walked to another truck to talk with a few people whose jobs put them in a position to know things the rest of us don't. I'd like

I surrender! What's for dinner?—A few of the 2,000 Iraqi soldiers at a temporary POW camp. They were ill-equipped, malnourished and happy to be alive

116

to know our place in the larger situation. I ran into a man who told me the following story: At the last stop, where all of us dug so furiously, this guy had to work inside on the trucks. He stuck his head out and told his workers to begin digging, since we expected incoming fire. Later, when it was time to move out and leave the holes behind, he stuck his head out again and asked if they were finished digging. Right before he told them that the hard work was in vain, one of his solders said, "Yeah, I'm done, and I made this one large enough for both of us." This man told me that never before had he witnessed such a pure gesture of love. When he told me who this soldier was, I felt the love as well, for he was one of my former "ghetto-mates."

February 27, 1991. It's 6:00 A.M., and I haven't had a chance to sleep. We're constantly moving, then stopping and launching missiles. The sun is doing its best to cast some light on the evil, morbid battlefield. I haven't seen anyone die, but I can smell it in the air. Missile launches are constant. Then, once in a while, silence covers the land—a dead silence.

Once again we are about to move on—this time to Kuwait. I was just thinking about weapons, how they're made and perfected so we can fire them with such ease, without a second thought. I wish as much thought were put into their use—and their making.

There was a lot of fighting through the night. We were battling the enemy, but we also had some confrontations with the terrain. That battle we lost. The moonless night made it impossible to see anything except when a missile was fired. Every time a missile went off, we used the flash to get an idea of our position. During the firing, moving and firing maneuvers our units became entangled. The potential danger of firing in the dark became apparent this morning when the light revealed how askew our formations had become.

There is something contemplative about squatting over a small hole, relieving your-self, filling it in, and carrying on as if that were normal. Of course, it's the more natural way to do it—we're animals aren't we? Even though we have evolved and adopted more sophisticated means of personal hygiene, we're still unable to solve disputes in any but the most primitive ways. It doesn't matter how elaborate the weaponry is.

The Iraqis were yanked from their homes and families and told to fight or die. Catch-22! Their only hope of survival is to surrender in the hope that we will treat them better than their own country. If I were in their circumstances, I'd rather surrender and live than die for my country.

Here we go again. The rockets are about to fly, so we grab our cameras and munchies, and climb on top of trucks to watch the show. We talk about everything from the war to our childhoods and past Fourths of July. Mindless of any danger, we mount the highest viewing areas to catch a glimpse of war. I feel like a tourist, sometimes.

After the show, I walked to the far side of my truck to urinate under the back tire. As I was half way around I noticed an apple juice carton on the side rail. I put the carton there myself more than four days ago. It remained standing through miles of rugged terrain. I took it as a good omen. It symbolized all of us. Who knows how or why this little carton stayed perched upright? Who knows the odds of its staying there one more mile?

Since, we've been in the desert, I've seen only two or three birds. As I sit in a battle formation facing the enemy, a bird has flown into my truck and sits beside me this very moment. "Hi little fella', Do you have a message? How far have you flown? What do you think about what we've done to your homeland?" He just flew away. He probably just wanted to rest and all I did was pummel him with questions. I would have flown off too.

Some Iraqi tanks tried to block us last night. We spent the evening and morning pounding them into oblivion. The radio said that more than 100,000 Iraqis have surrendered. How many never got the chance? How many are dead? I know our destructive power, and I've seen how we've used it. The dead must be in the thousands.

We're now a few miles from the Kuwaiti border—in a cease-fire, according to the radio. Still we sit with our radars on, ready to pounce on the slightest move or twitch. Moments before the cease-fire took effect, units all over the desert began shooting off excess ammunition. It wasn't enough that we used the Iraqis as targets during the fighting; they're also targets for ammunition we didn't want to carry. That's pitiful.

It looks as if the cease-fire will stick. We've been told to climb out of our worthless protection suits and get our first real sleep in four days.

There is one thing that those back home will never realize or believe. The allied soldiers have been fighting battles ever since we came to this place—battles against an assortment of elements: physical, mental, psychological. We are still fighting them, despite the cease-fire. Most of us are still living the war, fighting and losing it within ourselves. When you ask what we're fighting for, we reply, "Our sanity!"

120

PART EIGHT

There's A Joke In Here Somewhere

February 27, 1991. Too bad there's no land of Oz. Then I could just click my heels and say, "There's no place like home."

This war was easy in technological terms, but it's been psychologically devastating. Was it easy to endure death at every corner? Was it easy for thousands of Iraqis to die? Those of us who have experienced the war will never be the same.

We just received word to hang out and wait here in Iraq for a few days. We were told to set up camp, but no one is in any mood to settle in. We want to leave—soon. So, like scavengers, each of us is seeking out temporary shelter. I'm using the back of my truck. It's a bit claustrophobic, but I'll be fine. I'll be alone, which is good. We all want to be alone, though that's impossible with thousands of people so close together. We need time to contemplate, to make peace with ourselves for what we've just been through.

I was just talking with the driver for the Big Man, our division commander. The driver told us that yesterday, when the general learned that enemy tanks were blocking our advance, he told the driver to get on the radio and order the proper unit to commence firing—relentlessly. Even though he was under orders, the driver had second thoughts about ordering thousands of deaths. He gave the command after he realized that our troops would be in jeopardy if he didn't.

As evening makes its way across the desert, I'm sitting in my homemade hotel, waiting

I'll take perestroika and green peppers—Their bags packed, departing troops await transport to, of all things, a desert pizza parlor

121

to leave. If we don't go home soon, tempers will fray to the breaking point. It's already evident. Every day we stay here and do nothing makes the next day worse. Soon we will all go crazy or start killing one another.

February 28, 1991. For the first time in weeks, we slept peacefully. The war is over. I suspect many Iraqis are still living in fear across the sand, unaware that peace has been declared.

So now we have something to celebrate. I rejoice for the lives that were spared—mine first of all—by the rapid end to the conflict. But I still feel the unsettling presence of the dead out here. War! Thank God this isn't Leap Year. It would mean an extra day of this. I feel like a spectator to the conflict, hardly someone who can be called a veteran, though what I've endured was challenge enough. I can't handle much more. My mind is already breakdancing.

If someone ever makes a movie about this war, it shouldn't be about about the so-called glory of battle. Battle scenes are always dramatic, but they're secondary to the real story of the conflict: The fear and psychological demons you have to battle before and after the fighting; they're what this experience has been about. More Americans suffered death and injury before—and doubtless after—this war than during it.

We started taking malaria pills shortly after arriving in the desert—and soon began experiencing really strange dreams. We were told this was a natural side-effect of the medication. Well, last night's dream was a whopper! I was in a creek where I spent a lot of time as a child. I was standing in the water trying to place folding chairs in neat rows, but the current kept rearranging them. My frustration mounted as I struggled to arrange the chairs. Then, just as I was nearly finished, I saw many baskets filled with rotten apples floating downstream toward me. Then I awoke—strangely enough, with a sense of satisfaction.

March 2, 1991. This morning some friends and I toured the Iraqi side of the battlefield.

Non-turning turret—Another hulk, another victim of the withering American onslaught

I guess we were looking for evidence that the war had really happened. I wish we hadn't.

We drove for an hour, traveling in circles until we came upon a lot more than the few twisted tanks we had expected. Driving over a hill we came upon a scene that no one should ever witness. But we deserved to see it. We were the curious ones, we wanted proof. As we descended into this valley of death we all grew silent. There was nothing to say. Before that moment I never realized the full danger of my situation. Until then I could not imagine war's full impact.

Trucks, tanks, machines, people—all mutilated far beyond recognition—were everywhere as far as the eye could see. It was impossible to discern the individual identity of any face or vehicle. Unable to drive through or around the piles of metal, flesh, loose rounds, bombs and grenades, we left our truck to walk around.

We saw tanks that had been opened like tin cans; trucks still running, as if their drivers were coming back any minute; thousand of dead bodies littering the sand. They looked like toy soldiers scattered on a child's rug.

Some of our group hunted for souvenirs, I photographed everything I could. I wanted to record the truth. As I looked at the torn and mutilated faces, I could hear the screams, see the pain. It was the worst I have ever felt. I hated being American. I hated being the cause of what I saw. I was appalled, sickened, physically ill.

I snapped pictures of the wrecks, the remains of the passengers and their belongings, amazed at the way they lived, and nauseated by the way they died. No human being, no matter how he thinks or what he believes, deserves to die the way these people did. No matter how right we think we are, no matter how strong we are, no matter what we believe in—we had no right to do this. I'm sure that what I just wrote will offend some people. But remember, before you are an American, you are a human being. If you saw what I saw, you would feel differently.

The Iraqis' only military equipment were their vehicles, their weapons and some clothing. I saw evidence suggesting that some of the soldiers had changed into civilian clothes and tried to flee. I looked for diaries. I wanted to know what these men were

Deadly souvenirs—Iraqi troops left uncountable unused rounds, such as those for an AK-47 shown here, all over the desert in their hasty retreat

124

thinking up to the moment they died. I needed to know, but all I found were training manuals and copies of the Koran. The only food I saw was a bag of onions. There were no medical supplies or hygiene products. But there were enough weapons and ammunition to fight for months without running low. They could have fought and killed many of us if they only had had the will.

In one sense, these Iraqis may be the most courageous people in this war. They could have done much more damage and taken many more lives, but they didn't. They had no desire to defend their country, since their country had no interest in them.

I can't stop thinking about those soldiers. They were human beings, husbands, fathers. There must have been some who felt like me, who never wanted to be a part of this war and hated being in the army. They must have had dreams, hopes of being more than statistics on a battlefield. I kept thinking that I could be among those bodies lying in the desert with a stranger rifling through my belongings. I wanted someone to have a diary.

We've just had our first mail delivery since we crossed the border. The military finally saw some urgency in getting the soldiers their mail, so they flew it in by helicopter from Saudi. I got a lot of letters, all more than a month old. The first three started with "Oh God, the war is just starting, and they're bombing Baghdad!"

Since the fighting has ceased, I have had dreams of terror. Dreams were once my sanctuary, now they're a hell. I hope we leave soon. Every time I glance down at the sand I see corpses. Now that the immediate danger of the war has receded, I feel blank and empty. Why did so many have to die? Why not me? The next time two nations disagree with each other, let the principals fight it out and leave the innocent alone.

March 3, 1991. I've just heard that we are to move to Kuwait and take a border position tomorrow. There we'll remain until we're sent home. I wonder how long that will be. I find it amazing that our days here consist of so many activities, yet seem so uneventful.

March 4, 1991. This morning we moved—away from the front, rather than toward it. But we have to travel across an area infested with land mines. My fingers are crossed.

We're finally in Kuwait, though all of this desert looks the same to me. This time, when we received word to make camp and settle in, we did that and more. Tents flew from the trucks, and we poured all our energies into constructing living quarters. The tents are set apart from each other for privacy and convenience, not close together for tactical reasons, as they were before the war. There's even evidence of individual creativity. Personalized construction abounds—clotheslines, furniture—and this time every tent has its own pisser, which is a kind of privacy, I guess.

Rumor has it that 150 people from the division will be sent home in a few days. God, I'd like to be one of them. Every day in the desert is more oppressive than the last. Just when I'm about to lose it, I find or receive a book or magazine, or an inspirational thought occurs to me—one that lifts me far enough above the stench to let me breathe.

March 5, 1991. This morning I awoke at 0400 to pull guard duty. For some reason I felt a possessive zest for life. The day already has a strange aura about it.

This tent is my substitute home—shelter from the mischievous weather, which can descend upon us with almost personal vengeance. The wind and rain can be relentless, and the longer we stay, the worse they seem to get. It's as though they're telling us to leave, that we don't belong here. I agree.

March 5, 1991. Once more we're confined to our tents by the weather. It must rain more here than anywhere else in the world. Yet it's still a desert. With lots of time to think and no place to go, I have ruminated over my past.

I read an article about the drug and alcohol addictions of some of the great writers of this century. In my pre-Army days I had dabbled in these waters. Though I never used drinking or drugs to create art, I still enjoyed them. This war has several things in common with my previous drug use. The most important similarity is that they are both evil; if I had a chance to live these parts of my life over I would steer away from those episodes. So here I am in the desert—safe, thinking and breathing.

I'm as close to nirvana as possible out here. The others are asleep. I'm alone, and that is rare. I had a MRE for dinner, wet clothing, cold and damp surroundings, classical music on my Walkman and a full pack of cigarettes. It doesn't get much better than this. Somehow, it's great to be in these sorry conditions.

March 6, 1991. The past few days have been spent learning that we still know how to have fun. We're limited, but we're enthusiastic. The bad weather broke, and there was a game of touch football that turned into tackle. I sprained my ankle. I'm sitting on my cot in pain, but it was worth it. If I have to suffer, let it be from having too much fun.

March 7, 1991. Another day in confinement. New visitors arrive, bringing gossip from other places. We can do without it. We saw what rumors could do before the war, the fear they generated. Now we are already pessimistic about the length of our stay. We don't need speculation and recreational chatter.

It's 2130, past our usual bedtime. Normally we fall into bed exhausted, but there's nothing left to do. We lay about all day. Things in Hell are slowly winding down.

March 10, 1991. Here's a new twist. The wind has changed directions, bringing smoke from the burning oil fields. It's no longer possible to see the sun. It is almost noon, yet I need a flashlight to write outside. Day has turned to night. We watched the ominous darkness crawl over us. I'm sure that breathing is unhealthy under these conditions.

March 12, 1991. I just returned from a long search for a telephone. During the journey, we came across a few partially destroyed Iraqi tanks. I've already seen enough carnage, but everyone else in the truck wanted to stop and look. The vehicle was parked about fifty meters away. Everyone was careful to step in previous tracks to avoid land mines. When we were about three feet away, a tracked vehicle suddenly came speeding around the hill toward us. We thought little of it, until we heard the word Demo (as in Demolition). "Get away from there," someone shouted. "It has a Demo in it. It's going to blow up!" Forget careful stepping, we ran for the truck like demons. Everyone was in, except me, when the tank exploded. I was thrown inside the truck with tremendous force. Then the driver floored the gas pedal, and we flew over a series of bumps that were far more dangerous than a few exploding tanks. We had to stop and regain our composure before we could resume our search for the phones.

We've heard that as soon as a permanent ceasefire is signed, we can go home. Give it

Oil fires viewed from the Iraqi border—It wasn't until 1996 that the very last of these fires were extinguished

128

to me, I'll sign it right now. After that we'll either be assigned to the peacekeeping force, or we'll go back to Saudi, put our trucks and equipment in storage, fly out and try to forget all this.

The process could take thirty to ninety days. That would take us to summer. It's now getting hotter every day. By summer, I'll be able to mail myself home in a zip-lock bag.

March 13. 1991. You can tell the war is over just by the way we use light. In Desert Storm, we had to contain even the smallest beam, since any light could give us away. There have always been hundreds of thousands of soldiers out here, but you would never have known it at night. Now the desert looks like a city. The view leaves me breathless. From on top of my truck I see bonfires and high beams, glow-stick fights and even a few creative individuals tossing their flashlights in the air. It is a beautiful sight, the air is cool and breezy and my spirit is at ease. I feel well. Now get me down from here and send me home.

March 14, 1991. This morning we awoke with the day's boredom hanging over us like an anvil. So we looked for entertainment and wound up constructing a makeshift carnival game. We took three water bottles half-full of sand and a large ball made with heavy tape. The object of the game was to throw the ball and knock the bottles off the trailer. The fun lasted about twenty minutes. Now we're lying in our tents as bored as ever.

The latest news says that we are to move to the KKMC, bring our vehicles up to par, drive them to the port and fly home. When that will happen is anyone's guess. They say that once we arrive at the KKMC things should move quickly.

March 16, 1991. Oh great! We were just put on standing alert, meaning we could be called at any time to reenter Iraq. I don't need this shit. Apparently Saddam is slow to keep his promises. We might have to coax him a tad. Ever since this thing began, the allies have followed through on every threat they've made. I hope Saddam realizes this and listens.

The war's aftermath—Many GIs marveled at the total hell they had unleashed on Iraq

The boredom continues. I feel as though someone pushed my pause button, and I can't reach it. We are all on pause, waiting for a damn signature on a piece of paper.

There are several religious fanatics out here, and they're on the rampage. They search for weak minds to prey upon, attempting to convince them to join their quest. Every once in a while you can here the talk of someone who has just been saved. Saved! That's not appropriate at all. Confined is more like it. The question is: Who will save them from their saviors?

A few years back I was in the wrong place at the wrong time. To make a long story short, I had to spend seventy-two hours in the Philadelphia police holding tank. I was an innocent man shut in with about a hundred of Philly's most guilty breathing down my neck. The worst thing about the experience was not the company, it was knowing that as bad as things got for me, mentally and physically, I couldn't leave, not even for a drink of water. I told myself that if I got out of there alive, I would never put myself in such a situation again. Well, here I am. Same situation on a gigantic scale—for a lot more than seventy-two hours.

March 18, 1991. This afternoon took my daily stroll across the camp. I do this so my ass doesn't grow roots. As I cruised the camp, something seemed different. For a moment, I felt as if I were on a set from a Vietnam movie. It was the sound of the place, for since the war ended we're no longer forced to listen to music through headphones. Now we blast it out. This morning every radio played the same style of music—old 1960s tunes. It created a nostalgic mood that pervaded the whole camp. I liked it.

I got a bank statement today, telling me how much I got paid this month. I find it comical that this is the first month we actually collected the money we earned for being a part of all this. For risking our lives for our country and being subjected to the elements in this wasteland, we get paid an additional $150 a month. If I stay here long enough I'll be able to afford a psychiatrist.

The Army has recognized that we are beginning to sprout roots, so tomorrow will be the first of a three-day sports competition with all of the surrounding units. Terrific! We've spent the past months fighting the enemy, now they want us to battle each other to build morale.

Once again it's midday, and I am using a flashlight to see where I am. The smoke is thicker than ever.

March 19, 1991. I'm fed up with the Army's meager attempts to play with our minds. Today is Division Sports Day. We're supposed to play around, have fun and try to forget where we are. Then they tell us that in two days we're going back into Iraq. This is not subtle manipulation. The commander told me that the reason for us going into Iraq is that he has reservations at the Baghdad Hilton. There's a joke in there somewhere.

Earlier I was on the verge of freaking out, so my captain let me take a truck and a friend to the telephones. He thought talking to someone back home might help. It did. I called an ex-girlfriend and woke her up. We talked for about half an hour. The conversation was simple, but the feeling was strong. She said that her cat was lying on her back. I said that I always wanted to be her cat.

March 20, 1991. We awoke this morning to the sound of exploding tanks. The Army is destroying the abandoned enemy vehicles.

This is interesting. I heard an Iraqi general say on British radio, "If you break a snake's back you do not kill the snake, but it will begin to attack itself in a rage. And so is the country of Iraq. The Americans had the chance to crush the snake's head to kill it, but they didn't. Now Iraq must deal with the inner battle, as the snake attacks itself."

The oil fires burn constantly—and so do I.

March 21, 1991. 0100. We're awake because a big shipment of mail just arrived. They thought we'd be glad to get it right away—and they were right. We haven't had mail for more than two weeks. Now I have more than I've ever received since we landed in the Middle East. Most of the letters are from before we entered Iraq, but I love them just the same. I got a package from a girl in California whom I met through an Any-Service-Member letter. She sent toys and a stuffed animal for Valentine's Day, and a T-shirt. I think it's both strange and wonderful that the people back home are sending gifts. Surely such a thing has never happened in any other war. I wish I could personally tell everyone who sent something how special we think this effort is.

Change number 2013: We're not going back into Iraq. We'll stay here for seven to ten days, then begin the journey home. Whenever the Army has no idea what to do they say "from seven to ten days." My guess is we're not going anywhere.

Today I volunteered to help out with the mail. A bunch of people were going to another unit, so I went along to help. When I got there I ran into a soldier who told me some good news. He told me that because of religious conflicts with the Arabs, the Army was giving all Jewish soldiers three days of Passover R and R on a British cruise ship in Bahrain. That means me!

People in my unit tell me I'll be going at the end of the month—just a few days from now. Whoopie! I passed the word to a few Jewish soldiers, and they were delighted. The difficult part is sharing my good fortune with those who will stay here. We've all worked hard. Everyone here deserves R and R. My tentmates were a bit pissed but said they would feel bad if I stayed simply back because of them. I've decided to go. I feel a little selfish, but at least I have something to look forward to.

March 22, 1991. My tentmate, J.J., summed up the way all of us feel in two simple sentences. He slowly lifted his confused head, looked at me and said, "What the hell is going on around here? Are we ever going home?"

March 24, 1991. I thought I wouldn't have to pull KP after we left Saudi. Wrong!
Change number 2014: We're going back to Iraq tomorrow morning. It's supposed to be a show of force, because Iraq is being indecisive about signing the peace agreement.

One of my tentmates just got back from scouting out our location in Iraq. He said it would be near an old airstrip. He also said there are several large holes nearby filled with dead bodies and dirt. The entire area apparently smells like death.

March 25, 1991. We are back in my favorite country. The ride was interesting. We saw a lot of casualties—bombed-out buildings and oil refineries, piles of twisted metal that once were cars, even a dead dog or two. None of what we saw had much impact on me, which I see as a bad sign. Shortly after we reentered Iraq, I felt as if there was no air to breathe, as if we were on the moon. It sure looks like the moon, especially after all the craters we put in it.

March 26, 1991. The only thing that happened today was the confirmation that I'll be leaving for the cruise ship in two days. I'm a happy child.

March 27, 1991. One or two interesting things must have happened today, but the only thing that has my attention is the clock. All I can do is watch the hands move slowly toward the cruise. I fear I'll take one step on the damn boat and collapse from excitement. The anticipation is overwhelming. I once thought that the only thing that could generate this feeling was my work or the love of a woman. But the only thing that interests me now is getting on board that damn ship. What a crazy life.

136

Part Nine

"Get in da Cabin!"

*M*arch 29, 1991. Oh boy! I've had a crazy day, and I loved it. I'm on the boat, but before I describe it, I must tell of my adventure in getting here.

First thing this morning I was driven to another unit where a few envious good-byes were rendered. Because the majority of the people on this cruise are Jewish, we immediately named the round-up point the "Jew Holding Area." There we awaited transport to take us to the fun. I had already begun a friendship with an officer who seemed pretty cool, and like me, enjoyed being a bit separate from the rest of the crowd. We decided to try and arrange to be roommates on the boat. His name is Lee.

About fifty of us waited at that one station. Lord knows how many others would join us from other areas. Then the largest helicopter I've ever seen plopped down in front of us and we boarded. After the usual two-hour delay, we were on our way.

We arrived at Kuwait airport for another wait, this time five hours. After an hour-and-a-half flight, we landed at Bahrain. Then we waited another hour for one of the forty buses that had been sitting there since our arrival to move up and take on passengers. The short ride from the airport to the boat was strange, for this was the first time in a long while that any of us had seen a city. Yes, a city! The ride included a tour of the beach front, and an especially noteworthy event: stopping at a traffic light. Then everyone stopped talking and peered out the window at a car stopped next to our bus. A beautiful

Welcome to Bahrain—During an unexpected weekend of Passover R&R, Jewish troops enjoyed flushing toilets, a beer-belly/belching contest and other delights of civilization

woman was eating McDonald's french fries. I think I was staring more at the fries than at the woman.

But here I am, seated in a small, posh cabin with bright blue wallpaper and a green rug. I love it. The first thing I did was enter the bathroom and spend several minutes watching the toilet flush.

We were about to settle in when someone informed us that they were holding dinner for us and if we want any we must hurry. We hurried—to the biggest shock of all. For months, eating has been a dreaded chore. This was heaven—no lines, no MREs, just steak, shrimp, pasta, salads, cakes and pies. Amazing!

We were the only people in the dining room still in our scummy desert clothing. Everyone else got to the boat early enough to shop. We approached the buffet and began to shovel its contents onto our plates. I use the word "shovel" because it most closely describes what we did. At the end of this long line of food stood a man carving fresh roast beef. Then one of several waiters took my plate and scurried off. I was about to tackle him, but reason prevailed. He was just carrying it to my table, What a nice guy!

I sat down and noticed that Lee was having a similar reaction to his plate carrier. When he sat down, we exchanged a hearty laugh and dove headfirst into our mountains of food. Soon another suspicious character approached so we guarded our plates. But before we could tell him to get lost, poetry sprang from his lips: "Would either of you care for something from the bar?" Lee and I looked at each other as if we were having the same dream, then turned to the poet and said YES! Lee ordered three rum-and-cokes and I ordered three cognacs. The waiter looked at us and chuckled. I replied, "Who knows when we'll see you again?"

We ate our food and guzzled our drinks. Which leads to where I am now—on the bathroom floor waiting to see those same drinks again. I've been crouching here for half an hour. This time I showed some self-restraint. I only flushed the toilet about ten times. It's easy to tell that everyone is beginning to freak out, for none of us can remember how to act in the free world. I don't know what I want to do first—go swimming, see a show, go to the disco, scream, vomit or breakdance. I may pass out.

March 30, 1991. Last night we stayed in our room and talked about the good old days we didn't share. We were having quite a conversation when the door opened and a man entered—our third roommate—not a normal man but a drinking man. He looked more like a bottle of liquor than a human being, and he told us that his goal was to remain drunk until the moment he left to go back to the desert. He had a good start.

I slept for about two hours and was awakened by the lush as he left the room at 0800 in search of more booze. I had promised the guys in my tent that I'd get drunk for them. Promise kept. Now it was time to enjoy this place. I swear I won't drink any more on this cruise. The shops will open soon. Lee and I will try to find clothing that we like—anything that isn't green. We went to breakfast this morning. It was a replay of last night's experience with different food.

Well, we went shopping, though they had only three or four different shirts and three kinds of pants—all jeans. I wondered why everyone looked like clones. Lee and I looked at each other and laughed. He said we looked like hobos.

We put the finishing touches on our hobo selves and headed for the city. I liked the boat, but the urge to see the city was greater. It's holiday time in Bahrain, and you are not allowed to eat, drink or smoke in public before 1800. The bus dropped us off in the center, right in front of a Kentucky Fried Chicken, so in we went. Lee walked up to the counter and asked for chicken. The way he asked had me rolling on the floor in tears. We ate about eight pieces each and stumbled out.

Walking through the marketplace made me feel like a real GI. In Germany I looked like a German so I fit in. Here I stick out like a banana in a barrel of raisins. The people here are so glad to see us that they go out of their way to thank us in their broken English, as if I personally went to Kuwait and freed it single handedly. We shopped a bit and walked even more. It was getting close to dinner time so we went back to the boat. I wasn't going to miss dinner.

After dinner I went to a Beer Belly competition / belching event. Its object was to be the most obnoxious person on the boat, ensuring that if you won, you would never get a date. Ah, dating is an interesting subject. There are about twenty females and eight hun-

The main event—Contestants gather at the ship swimming pool for the belly-flop competition

dred males, and as a female comedian had vividly put it, "That's about eight hundred inches of dick!" Out of the twenty females, more than half of them are married, though that hasn't stopped them. There's only one I'd care to know, but for reasons I can't fathom, she is sitting with the winner of this grotesque competition.

We are an incredible mix of people from all over the States. Ninety percent of us are Jewish. The interesting thing about this is that we were sent here to attend the Holy services—and no one has. They announce services every morning, noon and evening, just as we're making ourselves scarce. Lee summed it up well when he said, "You must be kidding! I can't sit in a religious service for three hours twice a day. When would I have time for fun?"

I am now seated by the pool. Everybody is mingling, trying to make friends and plans. It's strange since there are so many ranks and types of people thrust together in this strange, temporary family. And by the way, this really isn't a cruise. The ship isn't going anywhere. There is a warm feeling, though, because for a few days we can treat each other as humans instead of GIs.

There's a man here who has everyone laughing at the mere mention of his name. You see, Army has a rank structure; those with higher rank are supposed to be respected by those with lower rank. Well, this guy—who's no more than twenty years old—struts around sporting sergeant major stripes. No one believes it; It takes years to reach sergeant major in the real Army. Our theory is that he was told to sport the rank because of his size. Basically, his presence discourages anyone who gets out of hand. He's like a big in-house bouncer. Another one of his duties is to get everyone into their cabins after the disco closes. He waddles through the hall shouting "Get in da cabin!" It's a sight. Imagine a very long narrow hall packed with drunks being shouted at by a very large man. It looks like a roundup at a cattle ranch.

Earlier today I entered one of the entertainment activities on the boat. There are many activities daily, and a small group of volunteers act as a morale-boosting team. They travel around the decks looking for people to play their reindeer games. This afternoon I was by the pool when they announced that the belly flop contest would begin in ten min-

Shrouded in mystery—Frankel as the Unknown Flopper, living proof of the human need to "run around like a fool just to let off steam"

142

utes. I wasn't particularly interested in making a fool of myself, but the prize was enticing—three extra days on the cruise.

Well, I am both motivated and crafty. I've witnessed enough of these events to know that the winner is either the woman with biggest breasts, or the person with the best gimmick. So I went in search of one—a gimmick not breasts. I had to release the tension that had built up in the desert.

I went to the front desk and asked for a big paper bag. I was thinking shopping bag, but the woman handed me a 50-gallon trash bag. Thinking quickly, I went back to my room and met up with Lee. Together we devised the Unknown Flopper. With holes cut in the bag for all the essential moving parts, we made a beeline for the pool, though we were late. Lee told me to wait behind the door, went over to the officials and had them announce the Unknown Flopper's late entry. The next thing I know I'm strolling out in front of a thousand screaming people. At first, I was confused. Are these people standing and cheering for this stupid Jew in a bag? They were, and I figured the contest was mine. Then it was my turn to dive. I was about three inches from the water when the horror of my situation hit me. Then my body hit the water. I flopped like a champion, but suddenly I was being dragged under by a soggy paper bag. I couldn't see, and I sure as hell couldn't breath. After long seconds, I clawed through the paper and lunged to the surface. There were loud cheers—for my gimmick and for my escape act. I figured no one could beat me. "I am the winner," I said to Lee.

Alas, it was not to be. Earlier a female contestant flopped in her bra, and her breasts were clearly visible when she emerged from the pool. I didn't stand a chance.

Tomorrow we go back to our units. This experience feels like a dream—even now, while I'm still in it. I plan to spend the last day doing everything I can.

We just returned from the city, where Lee and I were suckered in classic tourist fashion. We were sitting in a cafe minding our own business when a shady character approached us offering to sell Iraqi money—rare bills, he said. We browsed through the assortment and each chose a bill with Saddam's picture on it as a souvenir. We asked how much, and the man replied, "Twenty American dollars." Thinking, "Ah, why not," we bought our fabulous bills and then took them to the exchange. The man behind the counter gave a big chuckle. "Was the guy wearing a red coat and a gray jacket?" Yes. Well apparently he goes there every day and buys a handful of bills to sell to unsuspecting tourists. The bills are officially worth five dollars each, but they sell for three on the open market, because nobody wants them. I'm keeping mine for future object lessons—and laughs.

This last evening here has taken on a bizarre feeling, difficult to explain why. Tomorrow we'll all be sitting in the sand again as if this never happened. As real as all of this looks looks, it isn't. Tomorrow is real. This is just a dream. Ever since we got here, I've been a bit angry with myself for needing it so much. I never thought that I need to run around like a fool just to let off steam.

April 1, 1991. It's April Fool's day, and the joke's on us. We leave today. For three mornings I slept in a soft bed and pleasant surroundings. Tomorrow I'll wake up in the wasteland—with a slap across the face telling me it's time to pull guard duty.

We're standing in line while they make sure no one steals anything from the boat. We're hung over, homesick and angry at the humiliation of being personally searched.

PART TEN

Are We There Yet?

April 2, 1991. Well, here I sit in my good old tent with my good old tentmates in the good old desert. It's hard to believe that what I just experienced wasn't a dream. It may seem strange, but I feel much more comfortable writing out here in the desert. My thoughts are less inhibited. On the boat I felt as though my emotions were as chained to me as I am to this war. I couldn't describe what it was really like. The experience was too much, too fast—meant to be lived rather than recounted. It was what it was—a badly needed release of energy.

Morale around here has just skyrocketed. We've told to be ready to move back to the KKMC in Saudi anytime between tomorrow and the 11th. We could be back in Germany in mid-May. That word came from very high up and isn't just another rumor. People are actually walking lighter, as if anvils have been lifted from their shoulders. It's a beautiful sight.

I'm listening to the Indigo Girls on my Walkman and writing everyone I can think of, if only to convince myself of this wonderful truth: I won't be here the rest of my life!

April 3, 1991. I visited a few places today. The first was an enemy prisoner of war (EPOW) camp. As we drew closer, it was clear that we had found what we were looking for; concertina wire and machine guns were everywhere. We wanted to volunteer our

Eternal vigilance—This was one way to fill the empty days waiting for transport back to Germany

147

medical services, even though they shipped most of the prisoners out yesterday. We did this because we heard that there was a shortage of medical personnel and a lot of sick or wounded prisoners. On our way, we discovered a major highway—surrealistic after driving across so much nothing for so long.

But the real event occurred after we left the camp. Walking back to the road we encountered hundreds of women and children who had fled Iraq to seek the protection of the allied forces. As far as I could see, there were children in the arms of their mothers. They looked so hungry, tired, scared and hopeless. I went down to our truck to fetch some cakes and juices we had stolen from another unit. These people needed them much more than we did. I approached the crowd with my arms full of goodies and was immediately surrounded by kids. I handed out the packets, feeling better than any Santa ever felt.

Then I saw that there were more kids than goodies. I felt bad, really bad. I would have done anything to get cakes and juice for all of them. One moment I was feeling better than I have in months; the next, I felt worse—for just a few days ago I ate enough food and spent enough money to support every one of these children for a week. I can remember each small face. As I was standing there in my despair, I felt a tug on my pants, I turned and saw a little girl with her hands outstretched. I told her that I had no more food, she just shook her head and pointed. Then her mother came over to me and pointed to my camera. The little girl didn't want food, she wanted her picture taken. So I did, and you should have seen those little eyes light up when she heard the shutter snap. It was as if she knew that she had been captured for eternity. It's hard to describe how I felt—horrible and wonderful at the same time. I will never forget it. Never!

On the way out we saw a constant flow of refuges and prisoners all day—truckloads of people with nothing but the shirts on their backs. Their only hope for survival is us. Strange, huh? The only ones who can help them are the ones who caused all the chaos in the first place.

This day was probably the most interesting I've seen since my shoes first filled with sand. I interacted with people, the real casualties of this war. I feel as if I know a secret that most people here are not aware of. I feel lucky and scarred with each breath I steal from the air.

I returned from my little adventure to find everyone in high spirits, for we've been given exact dates of departure: May 2 or May 6, 1991. Boy, will these last thirty days seem to crawl!

April 4, 1991. It's 0145 and we have just been awakened by a bitch of a storm. I swear these storms are personal! It's impossible to sleep knowing that at any minute you could be running across the desert chasing your tent. The only thing we can do is hope—and hold on!

I have been told that I'll be going to the KKMC on the ninth. I'm supposed to drive the same vehicle I've driven throughout the war. I hope it makes the long trip back. It had the shit beat out of it during the war and hasn't been well recently. It can fall apart as soon as we get there—as long as we get there!

April 5, 1991. Well, things have once again been changed—this time for the better. I'm leaving for the KKMC tomorrow. I'm beside myself. Tomorrow can't come too soon.

April 6, 1991. I'm enjoying a short break from driving, leaning against the truck giving my mind some exercise and my ass a rest. We're on a road somewhere in Saudi, trying to figure out how to get where we want to go.

As we left Iraq, we encountered countless famished refugees along the side of the road that led to Saudi. They signaled us for food as we drove by. We were told not to give them MREs—not because we need them anymore, but because they cost money. Well, we figure they're worth a lot more to those starving people than they are to the Army. So our convoy looked like a string of Good Humor trucks, tossing ice cream to cheering children. It began with the MREs. When they ran out, soldiers started digging into personal stashes of goodies and treats. Anything and everything that might be of value to these people was flung from the trucks.

Finally, I had thrown everything edible from my truck but my lunch. Then we came close to the border and had to stop because of a backup at the checkpoint. I was just about to the break open my lunch, when a lovely, veiled woman approached, holding the cutest little girl. The woman motioned for food and pointed to her child. I looked at the mother and our eyes met. I was hungry, but I was going to a place with plenty of food. I

The real victims—The brief ground war devastated Iraq's civilian population. Here an Arab woman and her son beg in the streets of Messila

150

might not be there for hours, and I hadn't eaten anything since yesterday, but an incredible feeling came over me. I handed the woman my lunch without pause. The moment the food was in her hands, I felt better than I ever felt before. She said, "Thank you," and as she walked away, she lowered her veil and smiled. The little girl peered over her mother's shoulder and put up her tiny hand making the universal peace symbol. If I close my eyes I see that little girl's gesture and feel those emotions all over again. I hope I experience another moment like that some day. But if I don't, it's OK, for I will never forget this one. We're now at the last stop before the KKMC—unless we get lost. Shortly before we entered Saudi, we drove through Hell on earth. We came to a city that had been leveled by missiles. The bodies had been collected, but we saw the remains of thousands of automobiles, twisted beyond recognition. It looked as though the whole city had melted. Nothing remained untouched by the destruction. I'm not sure why, but we stopped for a rest right in the middle of it. As I stood by my truck, trying to understand what I saw, I heard my name being called from two trucks back. It was the division commander's driver. He was with us because the general was flying back later. I noticed he didn't look well and asked him what was wrong. He looked at me with tears in his eyes and showed me the map. "Look!" he said, "Look at those numbers—the coordinates! This is the place. This is the place, I did this!" I didn't know what to say, or realized there was nothing to say. I just turned around and went back to my truck and drove the rest of the way in silence.

Up to that point I had noticed that many others were feeling the emotional rewards of giving of themselves and giving food to the villagers. After we left that bombed-out city, I noticed nothing but how my mood had altered.

It's late. I am in Saudi Arabia about ten miles from the KKMC. Our camp consists of twelve very large tents lined up on a row facing a smaller row of latrine facilities. I'm the first occupant of my tent to arrive. As I tried to sleep, my mind kept replaying the day's events. I keep seeing the children risking life and limb to dodge trucks and retrieve packages of food from the road. I see the mother and child with my lunch, the face of my friend in the destruction he felt responsible for. I'm sure he's reliving the day and its

Survivor—Bedouins such as the man overleaf were a common sight in the early days of the war. Then they vanished when the shooting started and re-emerged after the ceasefire

152

images, wherever he is now. I will always feel the impact of these experiences. But I'm leaving. Those poor people have to remain.

Yes, we're leaving. I can see the anticipation in every soldier's eyes. We have just one step left before we board the plane. When we step off, we'll be on European soil. What a day that will be!

April 7, 1991. It has been a morning of reunions with those who stayed behind when I went into Iraq. We shared stories, though I did most of the talking. Everyone wanted to know what it was like. I stumbled through some anecdotes, but had to explain that it was difficult to sum up the experience. I still wasn't sure myself. One guy asked, "How was the war?" I said that it was fine except that there wasn't enough towels and room service. How do you answer a question like that?

Everything looks the same as when we arrived in this country five months ago. The sun is hotter and brighter, and the soldiers walk with lighter steps because we're going home instead of to our graves. The Army wraps you in a false sense of security. Its treatment lulls you into thinking you're worth something, then—just when you think you understand your place—the Army treats you like a disposable razor. I've been talking to an array of soldiers, from lifers to those who enlisted for a few years to get a little college money. All of them want to get out as soon as possible. We've all seen what the Army is really like in a intense situation. No one wants to be put in that position again. Life is too short to be a hero.

It's late. I've just returned from a tent with a TV and a VCR. The room was dark, illuminated only by the TV screen. We eagerly focused on it to fill our deprived minds. When the situation was comic we laughed, when it was tragic, we cried. It was our first dose of emotional expression in weeks. In the beginning, there were only ten or so people watching. By the end of the evening, there wasn't enough room in the tent. Soldiers were standing outside listening to the dialogue. We left happier than we ever felt in the desert.

Let me explain where we are, since almost every unit in the Middle East will go though a place like this on the way home. This place functions like a machine, pointing us all in one direction—homeward. Units come from all over the map to rest and prepare themselves and their vehicles for the return. Like territorial animals, our unit has staked out its turf and separated itself from the countless others who migrated here for departure.

153

To ease the pain of the wait, the Army has constructed a small city called the Town Center. The place consists of a movie house, pool tables, telephones and a free burger bar. It even has live entertainment on occasion. We're told that we can only go there on official business. My question is, how the hell could anyone have official business there? I told my boss that my official business for going there was to prevent insanity.

April 8, 1991. I'm sitting in the aid station with another soldier. Each of us was minding his own business until we looked at each other and screamed as loud as we could, "Boy, do I need to get out of here!" One of the things that makes me so restless is that we're only here because of the traffic jam. Tonight I almost snapped. I had a small temper tantrum, but I managed to confined it to a scrimmage with my clothesline.

April 9, 1991. Ever since we set foot back in Saudi, the heat and wind storms have escalated. Our days consist of sitting around trying not to dehydrate. Evenings are spent lashing everything down. Then morning again, and we dig out from the dunes that collected everywhere the night before. It's a vicious cycle with no end in sight at this point.

This morning when I was at the makeshift sink, scraping the layers of dirt from my flesh, someone asked me how I have been able to remain so optimistic through it all. I answered by saying that I have a goal in life, and I awake each morning to find ways to reach it. I was just thinking how grand it is to be out of Iraq. Even when the fighting ceased, our minds were under attack. We couldn't go anywhere unless we saw tire tracks ahead of us. No one was about to risk death in a minefield.

Since I've been in the desert I have reassessed the value of my life. It's hard to explain, but it goes something like this: My point of view has changed. After this existence in vast nothingness I can now hold out my hand, and even when I see nothing, I know I'm wrong. As long as I'm thinking, breathing and imagining, I will never be empty-handed. I discovered something in myself.

April 11, 1991. Nothing new except more preparation.

April 13, 1991. Ever since the end of the battles, Saddam has been firing on his own people—the Kurds. They have been forced to flee into the mountains where life is only possible at this time of year. Now the world seems to focus on their plight. Every time I pick up the newspaper or listen to the radio I hear that food and medical supplies are being sent to them. I always thought the most direct way to solve a problem was to eliminate the cause. Instead, we seem to be spending money, time and effort to treat the symptoms. The cause, Saddam, should have been eliminated when the opportunity was directly in front of us. Now it's too late. I hate politics!

I would volunteer to stay in the region if I could be guaranteed the assignment of going to the border and helping the refugees. I would stay to use the medical knowledge I've gained to help save lives—even though my fondest wish is to get out of here.

April 15, 1991. I just returned from the Town Center, where I waited for a hour to use the telephone. I called my parents and some friends, spreading the news that I would be returning to Germany in two weeks. I was moved by their excitement for me.

All the married soldiers are in the TV tent watching a movie made by their wives. I poked my head in for a moment, but decided it wasn't for me. I didn't think there was a plot, so I gave it thumbs down.

April 16, 1991. Today we were issued a full set of desert uniforms. Nothing like perfect timing. For five months we schlepped about the desert in our old green uniforms. When it's time to leave and be seen by the outside world, they give us the appropriate uniform.

April 18, 1991. While we count down the twelve days that remain until our alleged departure, the realization of how long this strange trip has been somehow sinks in. Since I've determined that I gained some internal strength from this experience, the next challenge is something I forgot in the process—the future. Now there's a subject I've not tackled for some time, and I have too little reference to even begin to comment.

The news media have been talking lately about how praiseworthy this war was and how quickly it ended. No one talks about the death, the pain, the destruction of the war. The military has made its details seem antiseptic—scooping up bodies, camouflaging casualty numbers and glossing over the conditions inside Iraq. The enemy has been left in a preindustrial condition with little capability for rebuilding. So once again, America will have to lend a helping hand and come across as the Good Samaritan. America destroys and then gives back to support its image. Who pays the price? The dead, the unborn—and us!

Some Americans are proud of this image of worldwide vigilance. I, for one, still believe in life, peace and the human race—not the "hippie" concept, but something spiritual. All this national self-congratulation seems to miss the point. The war was nasty; lives have been ruined—many lives. Let's get on with the rebuilding and stop flaunting our patriotism.

It's been getting so hot that people are showering in the middle of the day. They're not actually bathing, they're just standing fully dressed under falling water. This kind of relief is only possible until about noon. By then the water in the shower is only a few degrees from boiling. At times I feel like I'm melting. We spend half of our waking hours drinking fluids so we don't dehydrate. Then we spend the other half of the time urinating.

Most of the time we do nothing—for two reasons: It's entirely too hot to work and live, and we really have nothing left to do except wait out the traffic jam. Today, however, is the first day that I am sporting my new uniform. While I've never really liked military uniforms, this one is such a welcome relief from the drab green that the change feels good.

As I look down at my new uniform I am reminded of what I heard prior to crossing the border during the ground attack. I remember hearing that Saddam told his people to beware of those wearing the green uniforms. He said they were the ones from Europe who were trained as killers. I now find that as humorous as I did when I first heard it. I wonder if Saddam ever suspected the truth—that the U.S. military was too disorganized to give us the proper uniforms at the start of the war.

April 20, 1991. We leave in nine days. I am often entertained by watching how people have begun showing their joy. Some simply smile; others are going wild. Some dress in unauthorized garments and parade around camp. Some, married soldiers with families, seem to be walking around talking to their loved ones: "I'll be home soon, honey, so hang

Packing up—Many lawn chairs survived the conflict and, along with other essentials such as sunscreen and Chapstick, were shipped back to Germany

in there," or, "Daddy's on his way in just a few more days." It's a reminder that the married people will have more to look forward to than the rest of us.

We single folk will be greeted by empty rooms. Even so, I'll be anything but depressed.

April 21, 1991. I'm sitting in the Control Tent, for I am on ACQ (Acting Company Quartermaster), which means I have to stay up twenty-four hours doing nothing in an empty tent. My biggest challenge is fighting off the ZZZ monster, who will eventually win my consciousness. Earlier today I saw the biggest beetle I've ever seen. He was easily the size of a large apple, black as coal. I called him Darth Vader. He crept into the tent from under one of the flaps. I knew it was big when I could hear it enter. If he had wings he would have terrorized me. But I sat still and watched him stroll across the floor in my direction. I watched him until he got much too close for comfort. I sat there breathless, for in my still-morbid state, that bug symbolized my death. I watched him until he was an inch from my foot, then I squashed him. So much for dying.

April 22, 1991. Tomorrow morning I have to stand at attention for hours. There's a Division parade, and I have been volunteered for it. I hate the damn things. There are always high-ranking officers standing around talking about how we "kicked ass" or something.

April 23, 1991. Today we sat still, trying to stay alive in the blistering heat. The temperature is 115 degrees. They say it can get as high as 145 in the middle of summer.

The unit has sent a couple of soldiers to look for ice. Every once in a while, an ice-truck will pull in, and people swarm over it until the only thing left is wet plastic. The bottled water is running low, and they've sent us 100 cases of Perrier. I don't like Perrier even when it's cold; at near-boiling, it's terrible.

April 24, 1991. Today in preparation for leaving, we did another one of those useless police calls. We lined up and walked about four miles across the barren landscape picking up trash that has been blowing around the desert since Jesus walked the land. Desert trash collector is my newest skill. Others include foxhole digger, pots-and-pans scrubber, sandbag filler, cold shower endurer, blue-bowl clothes washer, guinea pig food tester, war tourist and spectator, makeshift latrine architect and, of course, shit burner. Do you think I can find a job? I have lots of experience.

I just got a letter from a lady I met through those Any-Service-Member letters. She has sent me more letters and packages than all of my good friends and family put together. She told me there's a history to her writing soldier in wars. This is what she wrote in her first letter:

> January 2, 1991
> Happy New Year sounds like a foolish thing to wish you under the present circumstances, but my wishes and prayers go with you in the coming year. There have been messages telling us that our service members would like to receive mail from us, so I am writing in hope that the messages are accurate and I can bring someone pleasure. I wrote a cousin in Europe during World War Two, a boy friend in Korea and another friend for a time in Thailand. This should indicate that I am not a young woman, but a mother. I am not a grandmother yet, but only because my child (a grown son) is still unmarried so I have not had the pleasure of spoiling a child unmercifully and getting even. Does anyone out there want to hear from a mean old gal instead of a gorgeous young lady? If so, I'm ready to pick up my pen again. This isn't quite like a dating game, but I suppose a little information about myself would not go amiss. Brief autobiography: native Californian, married, one child, one dog, recently left employment at Cal. State University.
>
> And optimistic I am, because I believe someone out there will enjoy my brief note and answer it. I feel like I have put my message in a bottle and dropped it into the sea. Who will pick it up and, if so, find it interesting enough to respond?

I wrote her back instantly, not knowing the barrage of letters and gifts that would follow. I guess she finally found someone to spoil.

I have often described the latrine facilities here in the desert. Well, the final chapter was written today. Behind one of the tents, someone had constructed a shitter out of tent-rope and cloth—the kind I had problems using when we first arrived because it's so public. Well, I was playing Frisbee with a few guys, and it was the nearest facility. I was sitting on the lethal chair, daydreaming, when the Frisbee crashed into my head and fell just inches from a messy grave. Everybody ran over, asking if I was OK. While I wasn't sure about OK, I was definitely uncomfortable with the crowd. So I quickly said I was fine. Then someone shouted my name. I shouted that I was OK, and please leave me alone. The voice responded, "We don't care about you. Is the Frisbee OK? If so please throw it out!"

April 25, 1991. This morning we had to shovel dirt into the trash-burning pit. It was more like piling dirt onto the pit, because it was so full. The reason for the cover-up: our division commander is coming this morning, and the pile is about 10 percent trash and 90 percent government equipment and supplies we don't want to schlepp back to Germany

April 26, 1991. Tomorrow the tents come down for the last time. Among our many preparations, the most important is private: the psychological adjustment to returning home. We've been in the desert for months. Sometime next week, we'll wake up in a place we'll actually like. Imagine for a moment that you woke up each morning to a day filled with fear and boredom. You too would find yourself living in the only available life raft— the hope of survival.

Already, people are letting off steam in the craziest ways. One man is wearing a pair of desert pants cut into shorts, a green army shirt with cut-off sleeves, one tan desert boot and one black one, no socks, a gas mask, gloves, and on top of it all a nurse's hat. I'm surprised we all didn't join him.

April 27, 1991. We were up at 0400 to break down the tents and prepare for departure. You should have seen it. Never before had these people jumped out of their beds so fast at four in the morning. The transition from full sleep to deconstruction at a hundred miles an hour was instantaneous. Tents were thrown to the ground, tent poles tossed about and personal bags were lined up like little soldiers. We rushed around packing, piling, pushing, pulling and arranging, until there was nothing left to organize. It had taken exactly one hour to flatten our makeshift city. We'll never have to touch those damn tents again.

Now we're waiting for the buses. I'm standing on the largest piece of flatland I've ever seen. Without the tents, we all look silly standing here in the middle of nowhere. All I can see for miles in any direction are two hundred men and four hundred duffel bags.

"THEY'RE HERE! THEY'RE HERE!" The cry turned everyone's head in the same direction at the same time. Off in the distance we can see a cloud of dust moving toward us. Everyone is jumping and cheering. And now they've arrived—four shiny buses, glimmering in the desert sun, blinding me with their beauty. We can only gaze at them right now, since, for some reason, we are not allowed to board. We pass the time discussing what we'll do when we get back to Germany.

162

PART ELEVEN

No Place Like Home

April 28, 1991. This certainly is no land of Oz. There's no yellow brick road, no wizard—and there will be no movement before it's time! At least 20,000 of us have been waiting overnight in a vast airplane hangar. I have a stomach ache from all the food I have eaten to keep my mind off the slowly passing hours. Some lucky people are sleeping. I feel like waking one of them and asking how he did it.

Due to the danger of bringing certain war souvenirs (toys like grenades and explosives) on an aircraft, we've been searched three times so far. Three more to go before we're allowed to leave. I don't really mind the precautions, but I'm tired of having to repack my bags time and again. Each time it seems that one more item will no longer fit.

Now we are in a smaller holding area. This one contains nothing but a few benches, and a TV playing the movie Coming to America. I've just been volunteered to load luggage onto the plane. I'm not thrilled, but at least it will be movement with a purpose!

The big bird is full, and my stomach is empty. But at least there's some good news: Since we loaded the plane, we'll be the first to board. I'll grab a seat near a window, positioned so I can see the movie without twisting my neck, near the bathrooms and, of course, in the smoking section. I wonder if they have an "extreme" smokers section. That's where I belong.

What's this? Flight attendants! There is a God! It has been so long since I've seen women like this: tall, thin—definitely more feminine than a drill sergeant. And they aren't

Exeunt—Happy GIs head for the long-awaited flight out

covered in sand. The bus is about to tip over, because everyone on it has rushed to the left side for a better view. One of the two female soldiers on our bus just said, "Why don't you guys sit down and stop behaving like men?" No sooner had the words left her mouth than someone bellowed back, "You're just upset because we finally have real women to look at, and we don't need you anymore." So much for equality in the military. It was a cruel comment—but not totally devoid of truth.

On the plane at last. I'm nestled in a seat, and the rest of the troops have come aboard. Everyone is smiling—glowing, beaming, ready to explode. My face feels like it's off the Richter scale. We're off! Now everyone is looking out the windows for a last glimpse of the place where we spent the worst time of our lives. As we climb, the desert gets smaller and smaller. Now it's gone, covered by clouds. The closer I get to Germany, the better I feel.

I fell asleep for a while. I woke up to the poetry of the pilot as he announced that we're over the French Alps. If we were to crash now it's OK. At least I wouldn't die in the middle of that desert.

Strange. The farther we get from Saudi, the more it all seems like a dream. The guy next to me has the same look that Jimmy Stewart had in It's a Wonderful Life when the little bell chimed on the Christmas tree. Some people are strolling around the cabin, chatting, trying to keep busy. Others are reading; the rest are sleeping. I'm sitting in the chimney section. It's like Pittsburgh at the back of this plane.

We've landed. Looking out the window, I see a row of German dignitaries waiting to shake our hands. It's nice that they came all the way out here to welcome us back, but I think I speak for everyone when I say, "Get out of our way and let us get the hell out of here!"

I'm stuck in fast forward. Everyone is too slow for me. I flew off the plane, shook hands, grabbed a soda and took a seat while the rest searched for their stuff. Come on guys, let's go!

I'm sitting as close to the door as possible. I want to be the first off the bus—the first to be cheered, the first to grab his bags, the first to hand over his rifle, the first to get his boxes out of storage. I'm not sure where I want to go with such speed, but I want to go out of here.

We've passed many cars since we left the airport. Germans are used to seeing busloads of GIs, but this time is different. This time we're returning from war, and they know it.

They wave, honk or smile. Even these small gestures leave a sense of gratitude in my heart. For a long time, the Germans have looked upon the GIs as hoodlums—trespassers in a culture they don't understand. I exchange glances with an elderly couple and feel a difference. They have only a vague idea of what we're returning from, but they're thanking us, and that is enough for me.

I can't wait to reach our destination. We're so close! I want to jump out of my seat and shout, "We're here! Now I can start the rest of my life. Get out of my way." For tactical reasons, I keep my mouth shut. I guess that's why I've written so much in my journals. I've often felt like shouting unacceptable things.

The last corner turned, we can see our barracks. As I expected, there they are—women, children, friends holding banners: "Welcome Home!", "I love you, Dad!", and my favorite, "Where the hell have you been? I've been waiting six months!" The bus stops, and hundreds of faces press against the glass.

Whoopie! I'm safe. It's two hours later, and I'm back at my favorite cafe. It hasn't changed—the same view, the same familiar faces. Yet it feels odd to be here, maybe because I've seen so much. I became a different person in the war—someone I rather like. If I had been somewhere else—Paris, say, instead of the desert—would I be so disoriented? Probably not. Paris wouldn't have created such a passion for the simple pleasures I dreamed about for so long. Like this cappucino, I'm downing cup after cup in an attempt to permanently absorb the flavor I missed for so long. I'm an emotional wreck. My adrenaline is racing—or maybe it's the caffeine.

April 29, 1991. I'm sitting on a train, headed for Italy. Today has been a blur. I spent the night with my girlfriend, and though we were physically close, we were miles apart emotionally. The crumbling of our relationship, which began even before I left, is now complete. She reached out to me before the war when she thought I needed her, but I wanted to be alone. Now our situations are reversed. I want to tell her about my experiences, about how I've changed, but she doesn't want to hear.

I woke up at 4:00 A.M. feeling that there was something I had to do. I sat and tried to think what it could be. Then it occurred to me: I have to get out and do things—anything, everything! I have just been given back my life. "Don't just sit there," I told myself. "MOVE YOUR ASS!"

I went to my studio—my home—and spent a few hours picking through memories to remind myself who I am. Then something caught my eye. It was an art magazine with images of Florence. I've always wanted to go to Florence. Its spirit has always seemed to call me. But for one reason or another, I never had the time or the moxie to go. There in the studio I realized there were no barriers anymore—no wastelands between me and my dreams. I ran to the street, made a quick stop at the bank and a beeline for the train station. So here I am, chasing my dream—and doing it of my own free will.

Before I get too involved in the Now, I should record what happened when we got off the bus yesterday. I was strictly a spectator, but the emotions were overwhelming—husbands and wives in tearful embraces, hundreds of bewildered children. I saw a guy I had talked with on the plane. He had told me how excited he was to see his wife and new-born child. Now, they were about ten feet in front of me, and I could sense the emotion of their first moment together. They were holding the child in the air. He was looking at the baby like a present he thought he would never receive. I remember every detail including the child's little jump suit with a large sign saying, "From: Me!...To: Daddy!" I took one more look and turned away.

I wanted to retrieve my bags one last time, but I was halted by the Command Sergeant Major, a man who might have said three words to me in the two years I've been under his command. He ignored my proffered handshake and gave me an enormous hug. I had always thought of him as the coolest military type I'd ever met, but yesterday he radiated incredible warmth. He actually said, "Welcome home, my son!" And when he said it I really felt that was home. After the hug he shook my hand in proper form and walked away. I watched him as he greeted the other single soldiers who had no one to meet them. He hugged them all, calling each of them his son or daughter. And at that moment, it felt as if we were one big family.

Then I saw a familiar face—the man I had talked with on the flight out from Germany, the guy whose son had the Ghostbuster jammies. Father and son were both ecstatic.

Hide in plain sight—A Green Beret in desert camouflage fatigues, which were issued after the war. The First Artillery Division fought the entire campaign in green uniforms designed for a European conflict

It took a while to tear myself away. I needed to savor the moment. Finally, I led a parade of single soldiers into the barracks, where we joined a small party someone had arranged for us. There was food and beer and more posters with messages of love. Then I led another parade to the holding area where our personal belongings were stored—and where the lessons of the war first made themselves felt. Before we left in December, each one of us schlepped his own boxes down three flights of stairs to the storage room—alone. Instead of helping each other, we were usually in each other's way. The process took days, when collectively it would only have taken hours. We must have thought we could handle this war thing by ourselves too.

In the desert, we learned how wrong we were—we couldn't have survived without each other. Now we had a wall of boxes to move, and without a second thought, we attacked the wall together. We were all in a hurry, but not one soldier opened his personal possessions until all the boxes were moved. When we finished, we looked at each other with expressions that seemed to say, "Do you believe what we just did?"

Funny. Those scenes are already beginning to fade. Sitting here in the rosy dawn of my new life, my memories of the past 24 hours come in flashes—walking, smoking, singing, smiling—and, oh yes, skipping. I remember skipping.

REFERENCES

1. Jacques-Yves Cousteau, *What a Piece of Work Is Man*; 2. Guy de Maupassant, *Les Dimauches*; 3. Jean-Jacques Rousseau, *Emile*; 4. Leonardo DaVinci, *The Note Books of Leonardo DaVinci*; 5. DaVinci op cit.; 6. John Fowles, *The Magus*; 7. Source unknown; 8. James Branch Cabell, *The Silver Stallion*, 1926; 9. Source unknown; 10. Alain (Emile-Auguste Chartier), *Histoire de mes pensées*, 1951; 11. Source unknown; 12. Source unknown; 13. Source unknown

Epilogue

A letter received by the author on July 24, 1997 from the Office of the Secretary of Defense.

Dear Gulf War Veteran:

I am sending this letter because we have determined that your unit was near Khamisiyah, Iraq in early March 1991. My purpose is to update you on our investigation of the U.S. demolitions of Iraqi weapons at Khamisiyah and what this may mean for you.

When rockets were destroyed in the pit area at Khamisiyah on March 10, 1991, the nerve agents sarin and cyclosarin may have been released into the air. If you were with your unit at this time, *you may have been in an area where exposure to a very low level of nerve agents was possible. However, our analysis shows that the exposure levels would have been too low to activate chemical alarms or to cause any symptoms at the time.*

Although little is known about the long-term effects from a brief, low level exposure to nerve agents, the current medical evidence indicates that long-term health problems are unlikely. Because the scientific evidence is limited, the Department of Defense and the Department of Veterans Affairs are committed to gaining a better understanding of the potential health effects of brief, low level nerve agent exposures, and they have funded several projects to learn more about them.

If you have health concerns which might be related to your Gulf War service, you are encouraged to enroll in the DoD Comprehensive Clinical Evaluation Program by calling 1-800-796-9699, or the Department of Veterans Affairs Persian Gulf Registry, 1-800-749-8387. Because there are many possible medical reasons for most symptoms, if you have health concerns you are encouraged to request a medical evaluation. If you have already received a registry examination and you continue to have health concerns, you should contact your closest military treatment facility or VA medical center to schedule a follow-up appointment. Please feel free to share this letter with your personal physician. If you are healthy and not experiencing any symptoms, there is no need for you to seek medical attention.

The health of Gulf War veterans is extremely important to us. The DoD and VA are committed to providing the best possible medical care to all veterans and equally committed to gaining a full understanding of all the possible health effects of service during the war. As we learn more about the events during the Gulf War, we will continue to keep veterans informed.

Sincerely,
Bernard Rostker,
Special Assistant for Gulf War Illnesses